SOME *B*ODY TO LOVE

A Guide To Loving The Body You Have

Also by Lesléa Newman

Novel

Good Enough to Eat

Short Stories

Secrets

A Letter to Harvey Milk

Poetry

Sweet Dark Places

Love Me Like You Mean It

Just Looking For My Shoes

*Bubbe Meisehs by Shayneh Maidelehs: An
Anthology of Poetry by Jewish Granddaughters
About Our Grandmothers*

Children's Books

Heather Has Two Mommies

Gloria Goes to Gay Pride

Belinda's Bouquet

SOME*B*ODY
TO
L OVE

A Guide To Loving The Body You Have

LESLÉA NEWMAN

 Third Side Press
Chicago

Cover art copyright © 1991 by Riva Lehrer
Cover design by Riva Lehrer and Midge Stocker
Interior design and production by Midge Stocker
  Text set 12/13.5 Sabon
Printed on recycled, acid-free paper in the United States of America.

Grateful acknowledgment is made to the following for permission to reprint previously published material: "Ode To My Hips" by Lesléa Newman, reprinted by permission of the author, previously appeared in *Love Me Like You Mean It*, published by HerBooks: Santa Cruz, CA, 1987. "Ode To My Feet" by Lesléa Newman, reprinted by permission of the author, previously appeared in *Sweet Dark Places*, HerBooks, Santa Cruz, CA, 1991. "One Spring" by Lesléa Newman, reprinted by permission of the author, previously appeared in *Good Enough To Eat*, published by Firebrand Books, Ithaca, NY, 1986, and in *Love Me Like You Mean It*, HerBooks, Santa Cruz, CA, 1987.

Library of Congress Cataloging-in-Publication Data

Newman, Lesléa.
    SomeBody to love : a guide to loving the body you have / Lesléa Newman. -- 1st ed.
        p.   cm.
    Includes bibliographical references and index.
    ISBN 1-879427-03-6 (alk. paper) : $10.95
    1. Eating disorders--Popular works. 2. Body image.
3. Self-acceptance--Problems, exercises, etc. 4. Women--Psychology.
    I. Title.
    RC552.E18N48   1991   91-34617
    616.85'26'0082--dc20   CIP

This book is available on tape to disabled women from the Womyn's Braille Press, P.O. Box 8475, Minneapolis, MN 55408.

Third Side Press
2250 W. Farragut
Chicago, IL 60625-1802
312/271-3029

First edition, November 1991
10 9 8 7 6 5 4 3 2

For Marilyn Eve Silberglied-Stewart

Contents

ACKNOWLEDGEMENTS

This book could not have been written without the loving support of the Monday and Friday Noontime Girls. I would also especially like to thank Arachne Rachel, Felice Rhiannon, Janet Feld, Marilyn Silberglied-Stewart, Prudy Smith, and Anne Perkins for their love and support. Words cannot express my gratitude to Lynn Matteson for introducing the concept of self-love to me, and then pointing me in the right direction. Thank you to all the women across the country who have participated in my workshops; your healing has been a great inspiration and gift to me. Lastly, a huge thanks is due to my agent, Charlotte Cecil Raymond, for all her hard work and encouragement, and I thank Midge Stocker of Third Side Press for taking on this project.

WHO THIS BOOK IS FOR

This book is for every woman who has ever looked at herself in the mirror and responded to her reflection with anything less than pure joy. *(Did she say joy? She's got to be kidding.)*

This book is for every woman who has ever said, silently or out loud, "Gee, I really ought to lose five pounds." This book is for every woman who won't let herself eat that chocolate chip cookie but has eight celery sticks instead, and tries to feel satisfied. This book is for the woman who has a calorie counter ticking inside her head like a time bomb—the woman who buys the size 11/12 pants instead of the size 13/14, even though the size 13/14 is much more comfortable and even looks better—the woman who weighs herself every morning before and after she goes to the bathroom, and the woman who sucks in her belly while making love (yes, I've done that too).

This book is for every woman who has ever gone on the Weight Watcher's Diet, the Banana Diet, the Grapefruit Diet, the Drinking Man's (sic) Diet, the 1200 Calorie A Day Diet, the 1000 Calorie A Day Diet, the 500 Calorie A Day Diet, the Dr. Stillman Diet, the Cambridge Diet, the Pre-Digested Protein Diet, and any other weight loss diet. This book is for the woman who eats brown rice and tofu by day and Twinkies and M & M's behind closed doors at night, and the woman who fasts for "spiritual" reasons, all the while reveling in the fact that she is losing a pound or two. This book is for the woman who binges and then purges by vomiting, fasting, crash dieting, using laxatives and enemas, or exercising compulsively. This book is for the woman who does not eat at all.

This book is for fat women, thin women, tall women, short women, women of color, white women, Jewish women, old women, young women, lesbians and heterosexual women. This book is for any woman who wishes or who has wished that her body was a different shape or size, and if you were brought up in the United States of America in the twentieth century, that probably means you.

WHAT THIS BOOK IS AND ISN'T

This is a book about loving yourself. What does that have to do with eating and body size? Everything.

I mean loving yourself right now, whether you weigh 400 pounds or 65 pounds, or anywhere in between. I mean loving yourself with your soft flabby belly, with your thighs that chafe, with your Jewish-shaped nose, with your frizzy hair, with your upper arms that jiggle and your round behind that wiggles. Loving yourself with that weird little toenail that's hardly even there, your crooked teeth, your pimples at a certain time of the month, and your breasts that are two different sizes.

This book is about loving you. All of you, just as you are right now, even if you're stuffing fistfuls of popcorn into your mouth while reading this book, or interrupting yourself every third sentence to figure out how many calories you've consumed today or how much weight you're going to lose by next July.

This is not a book about how to lose twenty pounds in ten minutes or how to have thinner thighs in thirty seconds. This is not a book about how to lose weight at all.

Wait. Please. Those of you who are about to put this book back on the shelf, I implore you to bear with me just a little longer. Believe me, you can pick up any diet book in just a minute. They're a dime a dozen. The reason there are so many of them is that none of them work. You know this as well as I do.

You know you know it. Why not just consider something different? There is a story about a woman who walks down a street and falls into a hole. It is a deep hole and it takes her most of the day to climb out of the hole, but she does manage to get out and continue on her way. The next day she walks down the same street and falls into the hole again. This time it only takes her half a day to get out. The next day she walks down the same street and falls into the hole, and within an hour she has climbed out. The next day she walks down the same street and trips over the hole, but catches herself before she falls into it. The next day the woman walks down the same street and walks around the hole. The next day the woman walks down a different street.

This book is the different street, the alternative to the deep hole of dieting so many of us fall into. This book will not tell you what to eat, how to eat it, when to eat it, where to eat it and with whom. This book will not insist that you that exercise a certain number of days per week or tell you which vitamins to take and which clothes to wear. In short, this book will not tell you how to live your life.

We all want formulas; we all want to know the "right" thing to eat, the "right" thing to do. This book will not give you answers like those. Instead of focusing on what you are eating, this book will help you focus on what is eating you. It will help you get to know yourself, accept yourself and love yourself. It will help you trust yourself so that you will be able to make simple decisions like what to eat for breakfast (yes, it can be simple) and more involved decisions like what to do with the rest of your life. This book will help you learn how to nurture yourself. You will unlearn self-destructive food behaviors and replace them with patterns of self-love.

But will I lose weight? Maybe. And maybe not. You might even gain weight. I hope by the time you finish reading this book and doing the writing exercises I suggest, your weight won't matter. Instead of focusing on your body size, I hope you will be concentrating on living a full life, a life that includes nourishing yourself with food that gives you pleasure, rather than punishing yourself by depriving yourself of food.

ABOUT EATING "DIS-EASES"

I use the term "dis-ease" to describe the condition of a woman not being at ease with herself. As I mentioned earlier, if you grew up in the United States of America in the twentieth century—or if you are still growing up (as I am at the age of 32)—it was probably impossible for you to escape the message that there was something wrong with your body.

Our culture tells us there is only one way to be—tall, blonde, white, heterosexual, able-bodied, young, and above all else, THIN. If you are not all of these things (and chances are you aren't), then from a very early age, you got the message that there was something wrong with you. And since you knew you couldn't change your height or your age or your skin color, you were fooled into thinking you could change your weight.

I believe that our bodies, if left to their own wisdom, would grow into a specific weight (which would of course vary slightly according to the season or the time of the month), just as they grow into a specific height. We can't really change much about our body type. When I lost forty pounds, over a four-year period (which I will discuss in detail a bit later), I really was surprised that I didn't become tall, svelte, and blonde. Really. I know that sounds somewhat bizarre, but I actually correlated a certain number on the scale with a certain body type. My body type remained the same—I was and still am your basic short, big-breasted, curvy, zaftig, Jewish woman. If you want to know your body type, check out the women in your family. Your body type is probably similar to theirs (gasp). Don't panic. There are several writing exercises devoted to mother/daughter relationships later in the book.

There are basically three types of eating dis-eases, with an infinite number of variations within each category. Many women (including myself) fall into all three categories at different times of their lives. This is because the body, in its struggle to remain healthy, can only tolerate self-destructive behavior for so long. Then it rebels, and we are forced to try something else. The three categories are bulimia, anorexia nervosa, and compulsive overeating.

Bulimia is a dis-ease in which a woman eats vast amounts of food and then purges by either vomiting, fasting, crash dieting (1,000 calories or less), compulsive exercising, or abusing laxatives and/or enemas. *Anorexia nervosa* is self-starvation by choice. *Compulsive overeating* is a condition in which a woman eats vast quantities of food, but does not purge.

I am not going to spend a lot of time defining these dis-eases and talking about their warning signs, and physical ramifications. Many books written by doctors, psychiatrists, and therapists already do that, and you've probably read many, if not all of them by now. More importantly, I believe these conditions are really symptoms of a larger, more serious disease, and that is what needs to be addressed.

It's sort of like talking about how to blow your nose when you have a cold. I could tell you to blow your nose with a soft handkerchief instead of harsh paper towels. I could tell you to blow your nose one nostril at a time instead of both at once, but until you take care of your cold, you're still going to have a runny nose.

What is she talking about? I believe that anorexia nervosa, bulimia, and compulsive overeating are all symptoms of a dis-ease that has reached epidemic proportions among women in this country. That dis-ease is called *self-hate*. No matter how old you are, no matter how much of a feminist you are, if you look in the mirror and respond with anything less than pure joy when you gaze at the reflection of your own unique gorgeous self—you've got it. The dis-ease of self-hate. It's in all of us.

We are not born hating ourselves. Quite the contrary. Self-love is our birthright. Can you imagine a little baby girl, five months old, saying to herself (if she could talk, that is), "Gee, I wish I wasn't such a chubbette. Look at these rolls of fat on my arms. Look at these fat little legs. I better do something about this quick." Sounds pretty bizarre, right? Why is it any different when a 7-year-old says it, or a 17-year-old, or a 68-year-old?

I believe that we are born loving ourselves completely. Try to imagine yourself as an infant, rolling around on the floor, completely enthralled with your ten fingers and ten toes, your chubby legs, your round belly. You know you are the most special, the most beautiful baby in the whole world. Watch yourself growing older, learning to walk and talk and play, taking your place in the world. Sooner or later, someone or something tells you there is something wrong with your body. You may be 2 or 5 or 8 or 12 or 17. It may be your mother, your father, your brother, or your sister. It may be some kids at school or some men on the street. It may be a doctor or a teacher or a bus driver or a bank teller.

The fact that complete strangers feel they have a perfect right to comment on our bodies, and furthermore that they are doing something of service, continues to amaze me. It may been a TV commercial or a magazine ad, but somehow you got the message that you don't look "right." And because we live in a woman-hating society, most of us don't have the inner resources to say, "Wait a minute. There's nothing wrong with me. There's something wrong with the message here." Or, less politely (for I don't believe that women should necessarily be "nice"), "Screw you. I'm perfectly fine the way I am and if you don't like it, that's your problem." Most of us respond by saying, "You're right. My thighs are too big. My belly is too round. I've got to do something about this. Better go on a diet."

That's the moment you become a sad little girl full of self-hate, instead of a happy little girl full of self-love. This book will help you heal that little girl inside of you (we all have one) and give you back the joy and self-love you deserve. It should never have been taken away from you in the first place. It's hard work to get it back, but you are worth it. Believe me. Even if you don't believe it, I do. Give it a try. After all, as I'm sure you've heard many times before, what have you got to lose?

MY STORY

If I were reading this book, I would want to know who this author thinks she is, telling me that diets don't work, telling me that I have to love myself just as I am right now. Who is she kidding? She doesn't know what it's like to walk into a clothing store and have the saleswoman roll her eyes in disgust. She doesn't know what it's like to walk down the street and hear a 12-year-old jerk sing out, "Fatty, fatty, two by four. Can't get your ass through the door." She doesn't know what it's like to spend two hours trying to figure out which apple from the fruit bowl is two inches in diameter, and thus has only 80 calories in it. She doesn't know what it's like to devour a whole box of Oreo cookies, a gallon of chocolate chip ice cream, a two-pound bag of peanut M&M's, twelve Ring Dings, and a large bag of Fritos in front of the TV on a Saturday night. She doesn't know what it's like to consume nothing at all but diet soda and black coffee for two whole weeks and still not lose enough weight. She doesn't know what it's like.

I do know. I know only too well. All of the above has happened to me, and I could fill a whole book with other such stories. But that's not really what I want to talk about. I want to tell you some other things about myself.

I am a second generation Ashkenazie Jew, born in 1955 in Brooklyn, New York. Because my grandparents were poor immigrants to this country, and my parents grew up poor and working-class, food was very important when I was growing up, as it is in most Jewish families anyway. All of the holidays were celebrated with certain foods, which often took most of the day to prepare. I helped my mother and my grandmother in the kitchen, while my father and brother watched TV or read newspapers in the den.

My first memory about food occurred when I was five years old. I was standing outside of Gussie's Candy Store on Brighton 4th Street with a chocolate malted in one hand and a pretzel stick in the other. One of my aunts laughed at me and said, "Look, she doesn't know which to eat first." I laughed too, but something inside me didn't feel quite right.

We moved to Long Island when I was eight years old and had two brothers, one two years older than I, and one four years younger. When we all got home from school, my brothers were given milk and cookies; I got carrot sticks and skim milk. I began to learn that it was okay for boys to grow big and strong, but not girls. Naturally, in response to this, I began to sneak my brothers' cookies whenever I could. I'm sure if I had been allowed to eat cookies, I probably would have eaten a few, and then forgotten all about it. But as anyone who has ever raised a kid (or been a kid) knows, a child always wants what is forbidden to her.

When I started developing hips and breasts, my parents took me to a doctor who put me on thyroid medication so I wouldn't get fat. I stayed on this medication and often abused it until I was 24. (If one pill would speed up my metabolism, why not take 2 or 3, or 10?)

I started my dieting career during my adolescence. I started moderately with a 1200-calorie-a-day diet. I bought a calorie counter, a little postage scale to measure out six ounces of lean chicken meat, and measuring cups to portion out exactly half a cup of unsweetened applesauce (50 calories). Instead of playing with my friends, I learned to make fake milk shakes out of skim milk and diet soda, which were really 90-percent ice cubes and air. I learned how to boil down tomato juice for hours until it thickened, and serve it over bean sprouts, which then became "mock spaghetti." If I was going to eat 1200 calories a day, I was going to make the most of each and every calorie. I would eat a whole head of cabbage in an evening and not worry because it contained less than 100 calories. But oh, my aching belly!

Eventually I would rebel, and be back into my brothers' cookies again, and anything else I could get my hands on. By this time (I was about 15), the whole family—in fact the whole neighborhood—was on to my dieting. I remember being invited to my best friend's house for supper, and her mother calling my mother to see if it was okay to serve me macaroni and cheese (it wasn't). I remember walking home from school eating a jelly apple, making sure of course to finish it at least three blocks before I even got within sight of my house. I walked in the door and my mother's first words were, "Your aunt Sophie called and said she saw you shtuppinz yourself—with a jelly apple on Forsythia Lane." (I do not mean to imply that my mother is to blame for my eating dis-ease; after all, she grew up in this women-hating, fat-hating culture herself.)

I went off to college, to the University of Vermont in 1973. Freedom at last. I could do whatever I wanted—go to classes or skip classes, smoke dope or take speed, participate in the "sexual revolution," and of course eat whatever I wanted in the school cafeteria. I continued my bingeing and dieting behavior all through college, noticing a few things. First of all I noticed it was harder to lose weight. Whereas 1200 calories a day used to work, now it was 800 calories a day. This eventually became 500 calories a day, then 300 calories a day, and finally 0 calories a day, when I discovered fasting. What I know now is that my body, afraid of literally starving to death, actually slowed down my metabolism, trying to hold onto my weight, despite all my maniacal attempts to get rid of it.

The other thing I began to notice was the different ways men treated me when I was "fat" and when I was "thin." (To clarify these terms—at my heaviest I weighed 185 and at my lightest I weighed 120. I am 5'4".) When I was "fat," men didn't pursue me in a sexual way, but when I lost weight they did. Since I was never taught how to say no to men directly, I would subconsciously put on weight so they would leave me alone. When I was tired of hating my body, I would lose weight again.

Here I must interrupt myself with a political statement. I believed at that time in my life, what I had been taught—that fat women are unattractive and certainly not sexy. I know now that this is a myth, and that the reason no one approached me in a sexual way when I was heavier was because I acted differently. At 185 pounds I did not wear flattering clothing, I did not go out dancing, I did not smile at people on the street. The message I gave out was, "I am a horrible and disgusting person. Stay away from me." At 120 pounds, I wore tight sexy clothes, I flirted my tuchus off, and I invited sexual advances. I had learned my lessons well.

End of political statement (for now) and back to our regularly scheduled life story. After college, I really didn't know what to do with myself. I lived in Israel and Europe for a year and then moved to Boston and worked at a variety of jobs. I was very unhappy, in relationships that never seemed to last long and in jobs that were very unfulfilling. But most of all, with my body which just wasn't the right shape or size and never would be, no matter how hard I tried. At this point I was alternating between bingeing and fasting, as well as going to a reducing salon every day. Having an eating dis-ease is very time-consuming—it's a full time job in itself!

I finally decided that where I was living was the problem, so I left Boston to move to Colorado and study writing. (Moving is also known as the geographic cure. It doesn't work.) I lost a lot of weight before I left Boston and felt that I was really starting over. But of course I wasn't. In Colorado some things were different. The mountains were higher. They served huevos rancheros instead of scrambled eggs for breakfast. But I was still the same. Still adding up columns of calories in the margins of all my writing notebooks. Still looking at my reflection in plate glass store windows, pretending I was looking at the displays. Still having rotten relationships and boring jobs. Still believing that to be thin and beautiful was the most important thing in the world.

After two years I moved back to Boston. I stayed there for nine months, spending one semester in graduate school. I was getting more and more depressed, my weight swings were more extreme, and my eating patterns more bizarre. One day I would eat five raisins. And that's all. The next day I would eat candy, cookies, cake, and ice cream from the minute I woke up until I literally collapsed.

I couldn't cope with graduate school, and I began to realize that I had larger problems than my eating behavior. I can't stress enough how serious eating dis-eases are. My condition totally disrupted my emotional and spiritual growth, as well as my career. I felt like I was falling through a large hole, a bottomless pit from which there was no escape.

I left graduate school and moved to New York where I thought I would really be a writer. I was terrified all the time—of the streets, the subways, the crummy neighborhood I lived in. I pretended everything was fine though, and responded to all the stress in my life by eliminating eating altogether. I lived on one quart of apple juice a day, with limitless amounts of diet soda and black coffee for six weeks. I got thin, so of course everything was fine. When I started eating again, as I inevitably had to, I started vomiting too. It was time to leave New York.

I moved to Northampton, Massachusetts, a small town of 30,000 with a large women's community. I had a friend there who said I could stay with her as long as I liked. I had decided the problems I was having with my eating was because life in the big city was too stressful and I was really more of a small-town type of gal. I also decided that no matter what happened, I would stay in Northampton for five years, which at the time, seemed like forever to me. Deep inside I knew I was running away from something, but I didn't know what.

Living in a small town was scary. In New York I could buy food in a different place every day. I could binge on the street and no one would notice (people do all sorts of strange things on the streets of New York). Here it was different. I could count the number of bakeries on Main Street on the fingers of one hand. What would I do once the salespeople knew me? Despite all my shame about my behavior, I was also terribly vain and went through all kinds of contortions to hide my dis-ease.

Needless to say, my fasting, bingeing, and purging continued, despite my new location. It really is true that you find yourself wherever you go.

I decided to start working with a therapist. During our first session I plunked myself down on her couch and said, "I'm bulimic. What are you going to do about it?" I sized her up and took an instant dislike to her—she was tall, thin, beautiful, wore stylish clothes, and looked like she had never been on a diet a day in her life. I worked with this woman for 3½ years. She assured me she had no interest in changing me. She told me I was fine just the way I was. I thought she was crazy. I wanted her to tell me how disgusting I was, but she never would. She offered me complete acceptance and I fought her every inch of the way. During this time I also joined a support group based on the principles of the book *Fat Is A Feminist Issue.** In that group, I learned how to listen to my body's hunger, not my mind's hunger. I learned to accept my body, and cautiously I began to wear colors one or two shades lighter than black. I even tucked in a shirt one day. Much to my amazement, nobody died, including myself. I learned how to give myself permission to eat whatever I wanted, even if that was ice cream for breakfast, chocolate for lunch, and granola for dinner—which sometimes it was.

Though I felt better, now that I wasn't fasting, vomiting, or dieting, I still felt that something was missing. I still spent too much time thinking about food. I couldn't tell if I was hungry or angry or sad or lonely. Or even happy. Any physical sensation seemed to translate to desiring food.

My therapist suggested I try a twelve-step anonymous recovery program. There I learned to feel my feelings and cope with them in ways that did not involve using food. I accepted the suggested structure of three meals a day with nothing in between. I could eat anything I wanted within those three meals. I did not weigh or measure my food, but trusted my intuition and body instead. That balance of structure

---

*   Susie Orbach, *Fat Is A Feminist Issue: The Anti-Diet Guide to Permanent Weight Loss* (New York: New American Library, 1978).

intuition and body instead. That balance of structure and freedom seemed to work best for me. After several years of eating this way, I was able to be more flexible and eat according to my hunger. Sometimes this means three meals a day; sometimes it means two meals a day; sometimes it means three meals and a snack or two.

Slowly food became less important to me. Putting it down was the hardest thing I've ever done in my life. I felt like I'd lost my best friend—the only one in the world who was always there to offer me comfort and who totally accepted me. As I adjusted to eating more "normally" all kinds of feelings came up—feelings I had buried by acting out with food. Some of the feelings were wonderful—I experienced a complete change in my sexuality and a surge in creativity which has resulted in the writing of eleven books for adults and children. Some of the feelings were horrible—I began having memories of childhood sexual abuse and felt very unsafe in the world. All of the feelings were terrifying.

What I learned, and had never known before, was that life is unpredictable. I can't control it. I think deep down, women with eating dis-eases are afraid to live as much as we're afraid to die. Maybe more. Since we can't control when we're going to die, we postpone our life. We put off asking someone out on a date, going on a job interview, taking kayaking lessons, or whatever it is, until we lose those 5 pounds (or 10, or 150). Then we never lose the weight, we never take the risks, and we feel that our lives haven't yet begun, therefore they can't possibly end. Yet all the while our lives are passing us right by.

When I was bingeing and purging or not eating at all, my life was totally predictable. It was exactly the same every single day. I'd get up, plan out my eating regime, blow it by the middle of the day, and beat myself up until I went to sleep. Yes, it was painful, but it was a way of controlling my own pain. When I gave up this behavior, I felt deeper pains much more acutely—pain from my childhood, the pain of loneliness, the pain of being a human being on the planet. It hurt much more than the guilt after a binge. But I also felt more joy than ever before. I began to know myself and to let other people know me. I found out I wasn't such a bad person after all. Some people even thought I was loveable. I let them love me while I was learning to love myself.

Now, eight years since I have acted out with food, I have a totally new life. I live with my longtime companion and run my own teaching and writing business. I eat breakfast, lunch, and dinner. I eat alone much of the time, but I also eat in restaurants, at parties, and at potluck dinners. Every piece of clothing in my closet fits me. (I finally threw out the size 7/8 jeans from ninth grade I had schlepped around for 20 years.) I have been at the same weight for four-and-a-half years without dieting, after losing forty pounds in four years, without trying. As a matter of fact, last year, when I started losing weight again after my weight had stabilized ten pounds above what I weigh now, I actually found myself feeling somewhat annoyed because some of my clothes that I really liked were getting too big on me!

I am not smarter, more creative, stronger, more special, or any more wise than you are. All I have done is decided to get well. I became willing to love myself. It is still hard work. I am by no means perfect. There are still days I look in the mirror and think, "If only my belly wasn't so big." These messages are very deeply ingrained in each of us. The difference now is I can say to myself, "Okay, Lesléa, your belly is the same size today as it was yesterday. This is a signal that something is bothering you that you don't want to face. What is it? Are you angry that your best friend hasn't called you in a week? Are you sad because a colleague recently died? Are you anxious about finishing the book you are writing?"

It's much easier to focus on a part of my body and start to hate it, than to look at what is really going on in my life. But now my old tricks don't work anymore. As a friend of mine says, it's like being in the Mafia. Once you're in it, you know too much to leave. Once you become self-aware, you're too smart for your own good. (My mother's been telling me that for years.) Eating 37 chocolate bars doesn't make me feel better anymore. The fact that I'm angry about my car insurance rate going up is still there, no matter how much I eat. I have to deal with my anger now, either by talking it over with someone, writing a letter to the insurance company, punching my pillow, screaming in my car, or canceling my policy. Overeating will not help the rates go down or change the situation in any constructive manner. It will only make me feel worse about myself.

It's really the day-to-day living that is the most difficult for us women with eating dis-eases to cope with. We can't stand being just one of the crowd. We have to be better than everyone else or worse than everyone else. I invite you to join me in being an average member of the human race. Try it, just for the amount of time it takes for you to work through this book. I dare you to discover just how special you really are.

ABOUT WRITING
AND HOW TO USE THIS BOOK

Why writing? I have been working with women with eating dis-eases since 1982, and I have found us to be a very intelligent, creative, and well-informed bunch. The women who participate in my workshops have read every book on the subject: eating dis-eases. They can quote statistics, recite the warning signals, and spout theories until the cows come home, yet they cannot stop their own self-destructive behaviors.

The act of writing cuts through the intellectual and theoretical, and connects with the emotional. It is very hard to lie on paper. The pen is connected to the heart. I have found in my own recovery, and with the women I work with, it is not very useful to "figure it out." Maybe you eat compulsively because you were never breast fed; maybe you eat compulsively because you were breast fed. Maybe you overeat because your sister was always thinner than you; maybe you starve yourself because your sister was always thinner than you. It doesn't matter. What matters is getting well now.

We women with eating dis-eases are great rationalizers. We can rationalize everything. Writing will help you get in touch with how you feel, rather than what you think, or what you think you should feel. You don't have to understand why you feel the way you do. It may not be very logical (feelings usually aren't). All you need to do is accept how you feel. Then you can make choices. As long as you're fighting with yourself, you cannot make intelligent decisions.

Women have used writing for centuries as a way to get in touch with and express our emotions. How many of you kept diaries when you were a kid or a teenager? How many of you write letters? Sitting quietly with pen and paper in hand is a wonderful way to get to know yourself.

The writing exercises in this book are designed to help you learn about yourself, to help you heal the wounded parts of you, and to help you love and accept yourself just as you are. Take your time with them. You don't need to show what you write to anyone (but of course if you want to, you can). This is for you. Not for your mother, your father, your lover, your therapist, or your best friend. You are not trying to impress anyone, or to prove anything to anyone. Not even yourself. There is no right or wrong way to do any of these exercises. However you do them will be the right way to do them for you. They don't have to be five pages long or written in complete sentences. I urge you to give yourself permission to write whatever comes to mind. Instead of having a preconceived idea of what you are going to say, read the instructions for the writing exercises, and then just write without stopping for the suggested length of time. Even if you don't know what you're going to say next (so much the better). If you knew what you were going to say, there would be no need to say it, for there would be nothing for you to learn. Try to be open to all the wonderful possibilities of your own heart and mind.

Don't rush through this book. As a compulsive person, I know I always wanted to lose five pounds in five minutes. Don't do all the writing exercises in one day, or even in one week. There are forty-one writing exercises in this book, most of which are followed by homework assignments. I suggest you do one or two writing exercises (plus the suggested homework) per week, and give yourself time to digest what you have learned. If you are someone like me,

who couldn't wait ten minutes for her dinner to
defrost before devouring it in three seconds, patience
is a very hard quality to cultivate. Twenty or thirty or
fifty years of self-hate are not going to disappear
overnight. The writing exercises will take you to a
deep place within yourself. You will find out many
things about you. You may not like all of these
things. That's okay. You'll learn to love yourself
anyway. Do you have a child that whines sometimes,
or a cat that scratches the furniture or a friend who is
always late? You may not like these behaviors, but
you still love the child, the pet, the friend. You don't
have to be perfect either. You still deserve to love
yourself.

Another way to use this book is in a group setting.
Women with eating dis-eases are often quite isolated,
as we tend to think we don't need anyone, we can do
it all by ourselves. Finding or organizing a support
group can break that isolation, and working with
other women who have similar issues can be
comforting, challenging, and inspiring. Start by
meeting once a week for ten weeks, focusing on a
different writing exercise each meeting. You may
decide you want to work with a trained counselor or
therapist, or have different members of the group
take turns acting as the facilitator.

Whether you work by yourself or in a group, you
will need to spend some time alone, writing. Buy
yourself a special notebook to do the writing
exercises in. Pick out a pen that you like the feeling
of. Start treating yourself like someone you love right
now.

Carve out a space in your day when you can be
alone, and really focused on yourself. Maybe first
thing in the morning, before the phone starts ringing
and the day begins is the best time for you. Maybe
right before you go to bed, when everyone else is

asleep and the house is finally quiet is the right time for you. Maybe you'll find you like to write in the middle of the day, or the middle of the night.

Pick a time and stick to it. Make your healing a priority in your life. Nobody else is going to do it for you. I suggest setting aside an hour a day, at least three times a week. Find a quiet spot for yourself—whether that's in bed, at your kitchen table, or in the woods. I suggest you really consciously fit working with this book into your schedule, rather than just catching fifteen minutes here and there. Err on the side of caution. Don't set up a schedule that you know is unrealistic for you.

For example, if I was going to start a running program, and I decided to run three miles a day, seven days a week, I probably wouldn't get out of the house. But if I decided to start by walking half a mile a day, three times a week, I probably could manage to put on my running shoes. You know your own limits. Set up something that is manageable for you. If you use this book three times a week, feel good about that. Don't beat yourself up because you're not doing it every day. It's time to give yourself a break. Focus on the positive.

If you decide to use this book three times a week and one week you only get to it twice, or even once, that's still no reason to beat yourself up. The Lesléa Newman Police Squad will not descend upon your doorstep and make you eat nothing but Lean Cuisine for a week. I'm going to be very strict with you, and insist you love and accept yourself, no matter what. Beating yourself up will not help you. It never has and it never will. Believe me, I tried it for 27 years.

Accept the fact that you are doing the best you can. You're making the healthiest, most self-loving choices you are capable of making at this very moment.

Every choice you make will teach you something and whenever you learn something there is success, not failure.

Please be gentle with yourself, loving with yourself, patient with yourself. Whenever you're ready, we'll begin.

HOW TO BEST MAKE USE
OF THE WRITING EXERCISES

All of these writing exercises are suggestions to help you learn about yourself and to aid you in your healing process. Not all of them will be relevant for every woman who works with this book. (For example, if you grew up in a single-parent household, the exercises concerning fathers, or mothers, may not apply.) You may find it helpful to read the instructions into a tape recorder and then play the tape back so you can close your eyes, relax, and allow yourself to really get into the guided imagery. Or you may find it helpful to have a friend or a therapist read the exercises to you. Please read them slowly. Take your time.

After you read the instructions, write for the suggested amount of time, without stopping. I suggest you use a timer instead of a watch, so you won't have to distract yourself by being your own timekeeper. Once you start your pen moving across the page, do not stop, no matter what, until the time is up. Even if you start writing things like "This is stupid," or "I hate doing this." If you get stuck, just repeat the last word you wrote over and over until you get unstuck. This form of writing, known as freewriting, will help you cut through the critical, self-doubting, rationalizing voices in your head that say things like, "I'm too old to write," or "I'm too young to write," or "I have nothing worthwhile to say," or whatever your variation on this theme is. These voices are not helpful. They only prevent you from getting in touch with and expressing how you feel.

Throughout the book after the instructions for the writing exercises, I offer some questions for you to think about, questions that will help you process the new information you have about yourself. You may find it helpful to answer these questions in writing as well. You may choose to talk about them with a friend or therapist. I also provide a discussion after many of the writing exercises also, as well as "homework" or activities that will support this hard and important work you are doing for yourself.

Please do the exercises in sequence, as they appear in the book, and do not do more than one a day. Remember, it's important to rest. Healing takes a tremendous amount of energy. Be especially good to yourself during the time you are working with this book.

THE EXERCISES

LETTER TO YOURSELF

Think back to the first time you heard about this
book. Did you see an ad for it, hear about it from a
friend, come upon it by accident at a bookstore?
How did you feel as you skimmed through the
pages? "This looks interesting." "Not another
dumb diet book." "I should buy this for my sister."

What prompted you to buy this book, to begin,
or to continue working on your eating dis-ease?
How do you feel about doing this work for the first
time, the fifth time, the thirty-second time? What do
you hope to achieve? How do you hope it will be
different this time?

When you are ready, write yourself a letter, telling
yourself how you feel about wherever you are in
your process of healing from your eating dis-ease.
You may not feel that your healing has begun, but
just the fact that you are working with this book
shows that it has. A part of you is wanting and
willing to get well. Look back on your eating
herstory in this letter, and tell yourself how you are
going to work with yourself to heal. Take 20
minutes to write this letter. Write without stopping.

AFTER WRITING

Re-read your letter aloud, in front of the mirror,
making eye contact with yourself. What did you
learn about yourself that you didn't know before?
Did you find yourself feeling happy, scared, excited,
lonely, resentful, depressed, or exhilarated at the

31

thought of getting well? Can you make a deal with yourself to work on these issues in a loving way? If you can, shake on it. If you can't, that's okay. Talk it out with yourself in front of the mirror, and accept whatever it is that you are willing to do.

LOVE LETTER TO YOURSELF

Write another letter to yourself (I hope you enjoy getting mail as much as I do!). In this letter you are going to tell yourself all the wonderful things you know about you, the things that make you unique, the one and only you. You are a gift to the world. The universe would not be complete without you, just as you are right now. So really blow your own horn.

Don't be surprised if this is hard for you. It is probably something you aren't used to doing, and maybe something you've even been discouraged from doing, or scolded for. ("Stop bragging." "You're so conceited.") Try calling a few friends and asking each of them to tell you five wonderful things about yourself. If they ask you if you've lost your mind, just tell them you're reading this really bizarre book and this is the homework you have to do.

Make it a real love letter, the kind you've always wanted to receive. Write for twenty minutes without stopping. After you write it, go over your love letter and edit out any criticisms or judgments about yourself (you'll be amazed how easily they tend to sneak in there). Make believe you are writing this letter to someone you really love, someone really really special, and imagine the pleasure they will get from reading it.

AFTER WRITING

Put your letter in an envelope and either mail it or
give it to a friend to mail to you in the next couple
of days. When your letter arrives, read it in front of
the mirror, making eye contact with yourself. Try to
ignore the voices in your head that may say things
like, "This is stupid," or "I don't believe a word of
this." Let yourself take in the praise.

HOMEWORK

Read this letter out loud to yourself every day for a
week, while making eye contact with yourself in the
mirror. Tape it to your mirror, or to your
refrigerator door. Write yourself love letters as often
as you'd like, and mail them to yourself.

GOALS

I.

Write down seven goals you would like to achieve in the next year. Some of them should be related to your eating dis-ease and healing, but they all don't have to be. Please do this now. if you can't think of seven, that's fine.

II.

Now find that voice in your head that is telling you you will never reach these goals. I'm sure it's there. We all have such a voice telling us we're too dumb, too old, too young, too fat, too whatever to do what we want. Right now, instead of telling that voice to go away, I invite you to let that voice run wild. Write for fifteen minutes from the perspective of this voice and let it tell you all the reasons you will fail. Write in the second person, using the pronoun "you" (for example, "You will never reach your goals because you are so . . . "). Write without stopping.

III.

There is another voice inside you. This voice knows you can succeed in doing anything you set your mind to. Everyone has this voice inside herself as well. Even you. This voice knows your strengths, your wisdom, your creativity. Spend fifteen minutes writing in this voice, telling the first voice all the reasons why you will meet your goals, and in fact probably even accomplish even more during the coming year. Write in the first person, using the pronoun "I" (for example, "I know I can reach these goals because I always . . ."). Write without stopping.

AFTER WRITING

Read the first piece of writing out loud. Who does it sound like? Your mother, your father, a sibling, a teacher, a boss? This voice is something that was taught to you. You were not born with it. Finding its origins and giving it space will help you destroy some of its power over you.

Read the second piece of writing out loud. Read it like you really mean it. Did you discover strengths you didn't know you had? Edit out self-doubt, judgments, and criticisms (they belong in the first part of this writing exercise).

HOMEWORK

Try writing a dialogue between these two voices. See what they have to say to each other. All of us have some degree of ambivalence about our own capabilities. If such a battle is going on inside of you anyway, it may be helpful to get it out on paper and look at it. Read the dialogue out loud. If you feel comfortable, have two friends read it to you, each of them taking one voice's part.* What

---

* If you're working with a group, group members can take turns reading one another's dialogues out loud for one another.

do you observe about yourself as you hear your
words spoken out loud? Which voice is stronger?
Which voice has more power? Which voice gives in
more easily? Which voice do you listen to more
often? Which voice would you like to start listening
to?

BODY IMAGE I

Picture yourself naked. Try to do this without any judgment. Take the time to really see yourself. Remember you have a front, a back, and two sides. Now focus in on one part of your body that you've always wanted to change. You may have wanted to make it bigger, you may have wanted to make it smaller, you may have wanted it to have a different shape, or you may have wanted it to disappear altogether.

Imagine that this part of your body has its own voice. It has feelings about how you've treated it over the years—the verbal and nonverbal messages you've given it, the ways you've punished it or ignored it or tried to hide it. Now it's this part of your body's turn to speak to you.

Write a monologue from the voice of this body part, in which it tells you exactly how it feels. Write in first person, starting with the words: "I am Lesléa's hips," and then write whatever comes to mind. Write for twenty minutes without stopping.

AFTER WRITING

Read this monologue out loud to yourself. How did this part of your body communicate to you? Did it yell, plead, whisper, scold, nag, whine, or try to bargain? Was it angry, lonely, proud, happy sad, scared, or defiant? Who, if anyone did it sound like? What does this part of your body represent to you? Is it connected with your creativity, your

power, your sexuality? Does it resemble someone in
your family? What secrets did this body part reveal
to you?

HOMEWORK

Do something loving for this part of your body
every day for a week. For example, if you chose
your feet to write about, get a foot massage, give
yourself a pedicure, buy an outrageous pair of
colorful socks, soak your feet in warm water after
work, draw a picture of your feet, make a
certificate proclaiming your feet to be the best pair
in the entire world. See how creative you can be,
and how much fun and how healing it is to truly
love yourself.

BODY IMAGE II

Read the following poem to yourself.

Ode To My Hips

Look out boy
these hips are coming through!
These hips'll knock you off your feet
if you don't make room for them to move.
These hips sway
these hips sashay
these ain't no size 3½ slim Brooke Shields
teenage boy hypocritical hips—
these hips are woman hips.
These hips are wide
these hips hypnotize
these hips fill a skirt
the way the wind fills a sail.
These hips have chutzpah—
they think they can change the whole world!
When I take these hips out
for a walk on the street
and the sun is shining
and my bones are gleaming
I place my hands on these two hips
and let them speak the truth.

Lesléa Newman

Write a love poem back to the part of you body
that spoke to you in the previous exercise. If poetry
seems too intimidating for you, write a love letter
instead (you've already had practice with love

letters in the second exercise of this book). This
exercise is a leap of faith. You don't have to believe
what you write, but write it anyway. Write a poem
or a letter in which you praise this part of your
body to the skies. Tell the whole world how special
it is, how unique it is, how beautiful. List all the
things it has done for you throughout your life. Tell
the world why you have the most wonderful,
magical, fabulous pair of legs, hips or belly in the
entire universe. How lucky you are that this
incredible gift does indeed belong to you! Spend at
least twenty minutes on this letter or poem.

AFTER WRITING

Read this poem or letter out loud to yourself. Read
it with confidence, as though you really mean it.
Were you able to write wonderful things about
yourself, or were you too self-conscious or shy? Did
you feel conceited, guilty, phony for praising
yourself, or did you feel happy and proud? Notice
how easy or hard it is for you to love and accept
this part of your body. If you feel comfortable, read
this poem or letter out loud to a friend or a group
of friends and have your listener(s) burst into wild
applause when you get to the end. You deserve it.

HOMEWORK

Hang this poem or letter up in your clothes closet
or tape it to your mirror. Read it out loud every day
for a week. Write a love poem or a love letter to a
different part of your body every day for a week.
Pick parts of your body that you like, and parts of

your body that you don't like. Who knows, maybe someday you'll be the author of a whole book of love poems to yourself!

BODY IMAGE III

Think of a part of your body that you like. If none
come to mind, try slowly observing yourself from
head to toe, until some part of your body calls out
to you. It may be the fingernail of your left pinky
or your teeth or your hips or your eyelashes. Take
five minutes to describe this part of your body and
what you like about it.

Now think of a part of your body that you don't
like. (Was that easier? It's okay. We all have a lot to
unlearn.) Take five minutes to describe this part of
your body and what you don't like about it. Read
these two descriptions out loud. Each part of your
body has a voice, and has feelings about the way
you have just described it. Write a dialogue between
these two parts of your body in which they speak
with each other about how they feel about
themselves, about you and about each other. Write
for twenty minutes without stopping.

AFTER WRITING

Read this dialogue out loud, or if possible, have
two friends or members of your group read it, each
of them taking a part. What did the voices of these
body parts sound like? Was one sad, happy, lonely,
angry, frustrated, nasty or defiant? Which body part
had more power? Which was more assertive and
which one gave in more easily? What do each of
these body parts represent to you? Did either of
them sound like someone you knew? How have

other people responded to these parts of your body?
Did you discover feelings of anger, sadness, joy, fear
or pride you didn't know you had?

HOMEWORK

Pay particular attention to these two parts of your
body and do something nice for both of them every
day for a week. Pick two parts of your body every
day this week, and write dialogues between them.
See what they have to say to each other, and to you.

BODY IMAGE IV

This writing exercise requires some "research." So put your pen and notebook down and find yourself a full length mirror in a room where you will have complete privacy. If you don't have a full length mirror in your home, buy or borrow one. (Perhaps you have a friend who would let you use her bedroom for a half hour.) Make sure whatever space you choose to do this exercise in is a place where you feel comfortable and safe.

What I would like you to do is observe yourself naked. Look at yourself in the mirror for a full five minutes. (Remember to use a timer instead of a watch, so you won't be checking the time every few seconds). Try to suspend all judgment. Imagine you are a beautiful creature from nature, or a lovely sculpture you have just chanced upon. Look at yourself from the front, the back, and the side. Look at all of you. Then write for fifteen minutes, without stopping, about what you observed and how you feel.

AFTER WRITING

Read what you wrote out loud to yourself. Are you surprised by what you wrote? Did you find more beauty in your body than you were aware of? ("Hey, I'm not so bad looking after all!") Or did you find the old self-hating voices stronger than ever. ("You are so gross, how can you even stand looking at yourself?") Or did you go back and forth between the two?

Whatever you felt is fine. Your feelings are useful information that you can work with. If you have someone you trust, talk to her about your feelings about your body. Ask her how she feels about her body. Most women, even the ones we think are "perfect" have ambivalent feelings about their appearance and their body.

HOMEWORK

Try observing yourself naked in a full length mirror every day for a week. See if you can increase the time you spend gradually, to fifteen or twenty minutes. Observe how your feelings about your body change over the course of a week. There is an old Zen saying that goes something like this: If you find something boring, do it for two minutes. If it is still boring, do it for four minutes. If it is still boring, do it for eight minutes. Then sixteen minutes. Then thirty-two minutes. And so on. Sooner or later you will find it very, very interesting.

Take the time to study all the interesting nooks and crannies of you. Do you know, for example, how many freckles you have on your left arm? Have you ever really looked at the nape of you neck? You are going to spend the rest of your life with you. You are worth getting to know. Appreciate yourself. Try writing a love poem to your entire body.

AFFIRMATIONS

Affirmations are a way of affirming self-love and belief in oneself. Creating affirmations is a two-step process. The first step involves writing down all the negative thoughts and beliefs we have about ourselves, such as "I am so ugly, everyone who sees me thinks I'm gross." Or, "My stomach is much too big." Take ten minutes to make a list of these kinds of statements which you believe about yourself.

Now here comes the fun part. To create an affirmation, pick one of your negative statements and write the opposite statement, or a statement that opposes the negative thought. Affirmations for the above negative examples could be: "I am so beautiful, everyone who looks at me thinks I'm wonderful." Or, "My stomach is exactly the right size it is supposed to be today."

You don't have to believe your affirmations. As a matter of fact, it's probably better if you don't (at least at first) because if you believed them, you wouldn't have to write them in the first place. Take each of your negative statements and write an affirmation for them. Make sure it is a completely positive and self-loving statement. "My thighs are okay, I guess" is not the idea. "My thighs are beautiful" is more like it. If you're a little bit unsure and uncomfortable saying your affirmation out loud, you're on the right track.

HOMEWORK

Affirmations can be used in many different ways.
Work with a different affirmation each day.

Try saying it out loud to yourself ten times in the
morning and ten times in the evening, while looking
into your own eyes in the mirror. Try writing your
affirmation in your notebook and writing your
honest response to it, until you believe the
affirmation.

For example:

My thighs are beautiful.
You've got to be kidding.

My thighs are beautiful.
They're as attractive as plucked chicken skin.

My thighs are beautiful.
Well, maybe in the summer when I've got a tan.

My thighs are beautiful.
*Well sometimes, when I'm sitting all the way
    forward in a chair and they look thinner than
    they really are.*

My thighs are beautiful.
*They do look good when I wear that black dress
    I have with stockings and heels.*

My thighs are beautiful.
Alright, alright already, my thighs are beautiful.

It may take you ten times or a hundred times, or
you may not come around at all. That's okay. Your
responses will teach you something about yourself.

Another thing you can do is make signs out of
colored paper, crayons, markers, glitter, etc.
proclaiming your affirmation, and then decorating

your house with them. For those of us who have taped our latest fad diet onto the refrigerator, or put up self-abusing signs saying things like, "You slob! Don't you dare open this refrigerator door again," seeing affirmations taped to the mirrors, walls, and kitchen cabinets can be very healing. You can also use photographs of yourself to illustrate an affirmation, such as "I am beautiful." Hang that on your wall with a gorgeous picture of yourself for a week (or a year) and see how that affects you.

We all know only too well the power of negative thinking. If you think you're too dumb to get that promotion, you probably won't get it. If you think you're too boring to go out on a date with so-and-so, so-and-so probably won't go out with you. Not because you're too dumb or too boring (you're not) but because of the energy and attitude you project about yourself. Try reprogramming these negative messages with positive ones. It takes practice, but it really works.

PANIC VS. PLEASURE

This is an experiential exercise. Before you write, prepare a meal that you really like. Divide the meal in two and set one half aside. Set the table with a plate or bowl, and utensils that you especially like. If you want, you can light candles or buy flowers for yourself. Create a quiet, loving environment for yourself, which will not be interrupted by other people, a ringing telephone, etc.

When everything is ready, sit down and take a minute to center yourself. Just breathe. Let the thoughts of the day come and go. Focus on now. Here you are, sitting at the table with half a meal in front of you.

Take a minute to smell your food. How do you feel with it right in front of you? Pick up your fork, or spoon, or chopstick and put one bite into your mouth. Now put your utensil down, and chew your food slowly. Close your eyes to really experience the sensual qualities of this meal—the smell, the taste, the texture. When you have completely swallowed this bite of food, take a second bite. Eat it in the same slow, deliberate, conscious way. When you finish your second bite, have a third, and continue in this manner until you finish what's on your plate, putting your utensils down between each bite. How does this way of eating make you feel?

Now put the second half of your meal in front of you. Pretend that you are on a binge. You are not supposed to be eating this food; it's not part of your diet. Somehow you have snuck this food into your home and you're all ready to eat it. But all of a sudden, you hear someone coming up to your door—a family member or a friend maybe, someone who knows that you are trying to lose weight. Quickly start eating your food. Eat it as fast as you can. Hurry up now, you don't want to get caught, do you? Shove the food in as fast as you can—you have to get rid of all the evidence. Make sure all the food and all signs of the food are gone—dirty dishes, wrappers, the smell on your breath, any trace of it on your face or hands, any bits of food between your teeth. Now you can let the person at your door in. How do you feel about that way of eating?

Take twenty minutes to describe both of these experiences and how you feel about them. Write without stopping.

AFTER WRITING

What feelings did these two different eating styles bring up for you? Were you able to prepare a meal for yourself that you really like? Did you create a pleasant environment for yourself? How did it feel to chew your food slowly and eat without distractions? Were you able to enjoy your food? Did you feel happy, scared, selfish, guilty, indulgent? Did you feel turned on? Were you able to eat the entire first half of the meal slowly and give yourself pleasure, or were you too anxious? When you were done with this part of the meal were you satisfied, or did you want more food?

How did you feel about eating in a rush, on the sly? Were you scared, nervous about being caught, angry at the intrusion? Did you get a rush from doing something forbidden? Were you able to get rid of the food quickly? Did it taste different from the food you ate slowly and deliberately? How did you feel when you finished eating? Were you satisfied or did you want more food? Write down your observations.

HOMEWORK AND DISCUSSION

There is no right or wrong way to respond to this exercise. Some women enjoy the first way of eating more—they can really taste and feel pleasure from their food. Other women feel too anxious eating in that manner; they are more comfortable eating the "binge" way—it's familiar and some women like the adrenalin rush that accompanies it. It may be scary to be alone with the food, with no radio, TV, book, newspaper, or other people to distract you. Many women find they are satisfied with less food when they eat in a conscious manner (though that is not necessarily the goal of this exercise).

When a meal has a definite beginning and a definite end, many of us feel lonely and somewhat sad after the food is gone. Because the meal no longer drags on indefinitely, it no longer fills "the void" that always seems to be lurking about—at the bottom of every bag of cookies, at the end of every chocolate bar. There it is—that lonely, empty feeling we try and try to avoid by filling ourselves with food or with thoughts about food. Once we put food in its proper perspective—something to nourish our bodies, a sensual experience to be enjoyed—food no longer works as a drug that helps us avoid our feelings. This is a mixed blessing, for though we will be more present in our lives and enjoy ourselves more, we will also be more present to experience our pain. A healthy life is full of both joy and pain. Acting out with food does not make the pain go away. It only postpones it.

Every day this week, eat one meal slowly, consciously, and deliberately. Set your table in a manner that pleases you, avoid distractions, and really focus on each bite. Many women say they never even tasted their food before they started eating in this way. You may find you don't even like some of the foods that you normally eat once you give yourself the chance to really taste them. Or you may find you do like some foods you weren't very crazy about.

Write about how you feel after you finish each meal. You may be surprised at how good you feel, or how scared or how lonely. You may feel a combination of these and other feelings This is good information for you to know about yourself. Often, when a woman with an eating dis-ease starts taking the time to nourish herself, very deep feelings of sadness come up, because she gets in touch with how frequently in her life she wasn't taken care of and nourished.

Allow these feelings to surface. Let yourself cry or yell or talk to someone about them. These feelings are a gift. They are part of your healing process. They will pass. The more you practice eating in a self-loving way, the easier it will become.

BINGE FOODS

Picture in your mind a food you frequently binge on. If you used to binge and don't any more, picture a food that you used to binge on. If you starve yourself and do not binge at all, picture a food that you would like to allow yourself to eat.

Imagine yourself getting this food—buying it, growing it, or stealing it. Watch yourself prepare it if it needs preparation, whether that means cooking it, reheating it, or merely unwrapping it. Now watch yourself eat this food. Notice if you eat fast or slow, with your hands or with utensils, sitting or standing, at the table, in bed, or on the floor. If you do not binge, picture yourself wanting this food and not letting yourself have it. If you purge, picture yourself indulging in that behavior as well.

Watch yourself clean up after devouring this food, whether that means washing dishes, throwing out wrappers, rinsing your mouth out, or brushing crumbs out of your bed.

After you have visualized this experience from beginning to era, write about it from the food's point of view. For example, "I am a Hershey's kiss all wrapped up in silver. One day I was just hanging out in the bag with the rest of my family when all of a sudden, a giant hand reached in and grabbed me, only me. I was very scared and the next thing I knew..." Recount the whole experience from beginning to end, from the food's point of view. Write for fifteen minutes without stopping.

AFTER WRITING

Read this piece of writing out loud to yourself.
Notice all the different ways the food felt during the
process, and ask yourself when in your life have
you felt the same way. For example, have you ever
been afraid of being swallowed up by someone?
Have you ever felt proud that out of a whole
crowd, somebody picked you, only you, because
they thought you were special? Have you ever been
afraid that somebody was going to chop you in
half? Have you ever been scared about being taken
out of a familiar environment? How this food feels
is really a mirror for how you feel. Think about it.

HOMEWORK

Write a monologue from a different food's
perspective every day for a week. Choose foods that
you like, foods you don't like, foods from your
childhood, holiday foods, and even foods you never
eat. See how different foods bring up different
feelings for you.

LETTER TO FOOD

For this writing exercise you need a "prop"—food that you either binge on or would like to eat but deny yourself. Bring the actual food into the room where you write and set it down near you.

Look at the piece of food next to you. Here you are alone in a room with the food. What feelings come up as you stare at this food? Continue to look at it without writing and without interacting with it, for five minutes. Breathe. Notice how your feelings change. Notice how your thoughts come and go. After five minutes, take fifteen minutes to write a letter to this piece of food, telling it how you feel toward it. Write without stopping.

AFTER WRITING

Read this piece of writing out loud to the piece of food in front of you. What did you have to say to the food? Did you have very strong feelings toward it? Did you feel more comfortable with it as time went on, or more and more uneasy? Were you afraid of it? Were you angry at it? Did you hate it and/or love it? Did you confide in it like a best friend, or seduce it like a lover? Did you try to make a deal with it? Did you try to make it go away? Did you just feel silly talking to it? Write down your observations and then decide whether or not you would like to eat this food. It is okay to eat it or to put it away for later or throw it out or give it away. Try to feel good about whatever decision you make. You know best how to take care of you.

HOMEWORK

Different foods bring up different feelings for all of us. When I eat kasha knishes, I long for my Brighton Beach childhood and the warmth of my grandmother's kitchen. When I eat celery, I sometimes feel mad, because I remember every diet I've ever been on. When I eat chocolate, I initially feel pleasure and then a bit of guilt. (I'm working on it. I told you at the beginning of the book I'm far from perfect.)

Write a letter to a different food every day for a week, telling the food how you feel about it. Pick different foods: "diet" foods, desserts, foods from your childhood, your favorite foods. See how you feel about each one.

DIALOGUE BETWEEN YOURSELF AND FOOD

Now that you've written a monologue from the food's point of view and a letter to the food, it's time for the two of you to interact directly. Pick a food that you like to eat and imagine it in front of you (for this exercise you do not need to have the food in the room with you). See the food clearly in your mind's eye. What do you have to say to it, and what does it have to say to you? Take twenty minutes and write a dialogue between yourself and this food. Write without stopping.

AFTER WRITING

Read what you wrote out loud to yourself. If you can, find a friend who will read the food's part, or two friends who will play both parts. What personality did the foot take on? Who was stronger, you or the food? Who was more aggressive, more passive, shyer, more assertive? Who was loving and gentle? Who was hateful or angry? Who pleaded, cajoled, demanded, threatened? Did the two of you get along, or was there conflict? Did one of you try to take care of the other, or "fix" the situation? Did the food take on a male or female voice? Did the food remind you of someone you knew? Did you feel more powerful or less powerful than the food? Write down your observations.

DISCUSSION AND HOMEWORK

Talking to food may feel silly, but it can be much healthier than eating food you don't want and then hating yourself. Often I have felt deprived because it seemed that everyone could eat more than I could (when I listen to my body, I do have a fairly small appetite). One day I realized I didn't want to eat the cookies everyone else was eating, I just wanted to have one, like everyone else. (At that time in my life no one ever offered me cookies or other sweets because everyone and her sister knew I was on a diet.) That day I took a cookie, put it in a plastic bag and smashed it to smithereens with my fist. I felt exhilarated! Often I tell women I work with, "If you're just going to eat this food and puke it up anyway, why not just flush it down the toilet directly and save yourself the time? Cut out the middle person. It's a lot quicker and a lot less painful."

Now you probably think I've lost my mind (wait'll you see what the homework is!), but I am very serious. I'd like you to get a food that you either binge on or would like to eat but deny yourself, and destroy it. One of the women I've worked with took an entire bag of M&M's and smashed it with a hammer in her driveway. She'd been eating a bag or two compulsively every day at work. After destroying them, she realized she didn't even like them! I myself have found it very satisfying to burn bits of Twinkies in a wood stove. After doing this homework you may feel quite differently about food. Write about how you feel, or talk to a friend or therapist about it.

This homework exercise may be scary for you to do. If you feel angry or full of rage, that's okay. Better to smash a bag of M&M's than to hurt yourself or someone else. If you get pleasure out of destroying food, that's okay too. It can be very satisfying to take the anger out on something other than yourself. You may feel energized as well. Anger turned inward becomes depression. Anger expressed in constructive ways and thus released is energizing.

We will be writing about and discussing anger later on in this book. And now a note to those of you who are rationalizing why this exercise is "wrong"—it's a waste of food, children are starving all over the world, etc. etc. I strongly believe that using food for emotional healing is not wasting it at all. M&M's will not help starving children anywhere, though of course nutritious food would. Many a woman with an eating dis-ease grew up as a charter member of the "clean plate club." If you are really concerned about world hunger, contribute time and/or money to the cause. Meanwhile, notice what feelings come up for you around doing this exercise. It is fine to choose to do it, or to choose not to do it. Write down your feelings about it.

BINGEING

If you do not binge, skip this exercise and go on to the next one.

Picture yourself on a binge. A full scale this-is-it-I-don't-care-anymore-I-hate-everyone-and-everything-and-I'm-really-going-to- do-it-this-time binge. Don't hold back. In your mind's eye, watch yourself get all those foods you've always wanted, and devour them. Take your time and be really thorough. If you purge, also imagine yourself purging after consuming all this food. Write a description of the experience you just witnessed, including how you feel about it. Take twenty minutes, and write without stopping.

Now I'd like you to think of someone you love very dearly. It may be your lover, your best friend, your child, a friend's child, a parent, a sibling, or someone else. Make sure this person is someone you care for very deeply, and someone you do not have any issues with at this time. (For example, don't pick someone you love very much but who you aren't speaking to because the two of you just had a huge fight last night.) Choose someone you accept fully and love unconditionally.

Imagine the same bingeing scene you just wrote about, but put the person you love in place of yourself. Imagine them bingeing on the same foods in the very same way, from start to finish.

Then take twenty minutes to describe what you observed and how you feel about it.

AFTER WRITING

Read these two pieces of writing out loud to
yourself. Notice if there were any differences in the
way you felt about watching yourself on a binge
and watching your loved one. Did you feel disgust
for one and compassion for the other? Could you
feel one person's pain more deeply? Who, if anyone,
did you want to comfort? Who, if anyone, did you
want to punish? Did your feelings toward yourself
change as you watched yourself binge? Did your
feelings for your loved one change?

DISCUSSION AND HOMEWORK

Notice whenever you judge, criticize, or get down
on yourself during the day. What messages do you
give yourself? ("That was so dumb. I'm such an
idiot!") Imagine what you would say to a person
you love in a similar situation. Chances are, it
wouldn't be the same thing. If we treated our
friends the way we treat ourselves, we probably
wouldn't have any friends! Do you really say to
someone you love, "You're such a jerk"? You
probably say things like, "Oh well, you made a
mistake. You're only human." Or, "You must feel
badly about that. What can I give you, a hug, a
back rub, a shoulder to cry on?"
   Try treating yourself as though you're someone
you love, in a conscious way. Next time you're
about to get down on yourself, say instead, "How
would I treat _____?" (the person you
love). Then treat yourself in exactly that manner.
You deserve it.

STARVING

If you do not starve yourself, skip this exercise and go on to the next one.

Imagine yourself not eating. Watch how you avoid food, whether you keep yourself away from meals, push food around on your plate, or feed your food to your dog. Imagine yourself waking up in the morning and going through an entire day, either eating nothing or eating very little, depending on the form your deprivation takes. Imagine yourself almost eating, being tempted to eat, battling with yourself about eating, or "flirting" with food, if these are things you actually do. Picture yourself going to bed at the end of such a day. Write a description of what you just witnessed and how you feel about it. Write for fifteen minutes without stopping.

Now think of someone you love very dearly. It may be your lover, your best friend, your child, a friend's child, a parent, a sibling, or someone else. Make sure this person is someone you care about very deeply, and someone you don't have any issues with at this time. (For example, don't pick someone you really love but who you aren't speaking to at the moment because the two of you had a huge fight last night.) Choose someone you fully accept and love unconditionally. Imagine the same day of self-starvation you just wrote about, but replace yourself with the person you love. Imagine them in your place, starving, from the beginning of the day to the end. Then take fifteen minutes to write about what you observed and how you feel about it. Write without stopping.

AFTER WRITING

Read these two pieces of writing out loud. Notice if there were any differences in the way you felt watching yourself starve and watching your loved one. Did you feel disgust for one, and compassion for the other? Could you feel one person's pain more deeply? Who, if anyone, did you want to comfort? Who, if anyone, did you want to punish? Did your feelings for yourself change as you witnessed yourself starving? Did your feelings for your loved one change?

DISCUSSION AND HOMEWORK

Notice whenever you judge, criticize, or get down on yourself during the day. What messages do you give yourself? ("That was so dumb. I'm such an idiot") Imagine what you would say to someone you love in a similar situation. Chances are it wouldn't be the same thing. If we treated our friends the way we treat ourselves, we probably wouldn't have any friends! Do you really say to someone you love, "You're such a jerk"? You probably say things like, "oh well, you made a mistake. You're only human." Or, "You must feel badly about that. Can I give you a hug, or a backrub or a shoulder to cry on?" Try treating yourself as if you are someone you love, in a really conscious way. Next time you're about to give yourself a hard time, say instead, "How would I

treat _____?"(the person you
love). Then treat yourself in exactly that manner.
You deserve it.

HUNGER

Women are hungry beings. We are hungry for food, hungry for love, hungry for satisfying relationships, meaningful jobs, adequate childcare, and hungry for respect. This writing exercise will help you get in touch with your own hungers.

Read the following poem out loud to yourself.

Hunger

Inside me
the hunger inside
the hunger inside
the hunger forever
like those funny wooden dolls from Russia
the hunger inside
the hunger inside
me forever
is demanding
to be fed

In the middle of the night
I wake to feed it
eating and eating until my belly
is stretched tight as the skin
on an ancient drum

Still I hear the cries
of mountain lions perched on my hipbones
small black bears clinging to the tree of my
spine
angelfish swimming in schools through my veins

And I eat more and more
until my thighs grow fat and get in each other's
way
as I walk down the street, like two women
in the A&P trying to squeeze by each other
their arms full of canned peaches
and hamburger rolls

And still the construction men
and the garbage men and the business men
wink and whistle and yell "Hi Beautiful"
as I pass looking for more food to give this
body
that can no longer be contained by skirts or
slacks
or sweaters and **certainly** *not by me*
and why couldn't they see

that the hunger inside me
is churning like a volcano
threatening to devour me
unless I keep eating and eating
and like a child's pet iguana
that will grow big enough to fit its cage
I grow big as the world
making the earth tremble as I walk
leveling buildings with each step I take
everyone running this way and that
trying to get out from under my great black
shadow
but there is nowhere to go

and still I feel hungry

Lesléa Newman

Take a deep breath and locate where in your body
your hunger lives. Does it live in your belly, your
throat, your head, your heart, your hands, your
hips, your feet? What color is your hunger? What
shape is your hunger? What size is it? Imagine that
your hunger has a voice. It wants to communicate
its needs to you. How does your hunger speak?
Does it growl, whisper, plead, nag, scold, beg,
bargain, scream, roar? What does it want?

Write a letter to yourself from your hunger's
point of view. Let your hunger describe itself to you
and tell you what it wants. Write in first person,
and write for fifteen minutes without stopping.

AFTER WRITING

Read this letter out loud to yourself. Does your
hunger sound like anyone you know? Were you
able to locate where it lives? Were you surprised at
its shape and color? Were you able to let it voice its
needs? Were you surprised at how much or at how
little it wanted? How do you feel about having
needs at all? Do you feel you deserve to have your
needs met? When you were a child, how did your
parents respond when you asked for something you
needed? Write down your observations.

HOMEWORK

At least once a day for a week, check in with your
hunger. You can do this out loud, or by writing in
your hunger's voice. Do you want a tuna fish
sandwich or a hot bath? Are you hungry for some
corn on the cob or for a good cry? Really take the
time to figure out what you need. This may take
some practice. You may not know what you need.

That's okay. You're just getting to know yourself—your own wants and needs. They are different from everyone else's. If you can't figure out what you're hungry for, accept that, and give yourself a pat on the back for being so honest with yourself.

Check in with your hunger later, or tomorrow. With practice, it will become easier for you to know exactly what you are hungry for.

NEEDS

Make a list of your needs. If you think, "Oh, I'm fine. I don't need anything," make a list of your needs anyway. Every human being has needs. Women with eating dis-eases often believe they have no needs, especially women who starve themselves—we don't even need food! Take five minutes, and come up with at least ten things you need or want. Try to be specific and realistic. For example, instead of saying, "I need a great car," say "I need to get my muffler fixed." Or, instead of saying "I need a satisfying relationship," say, "I need so-and-so to pay more attention to me."

Now pick one of these needs, one that involves someone else. If none of your needs involve someone else, modify one so that it does. If for example, you wrote down, "I need lots of money," modify that into "I need to ask my boss for a raise," or "I need to ask my sister if I can borrow $100." (Even if this is unrealistic, it is still good practice.) Imagine yourself asking this person for what you need. Notice how you prepare to ask, the manner in which you ask and how you respond to the answer you receive. Take fifteen minutes to write down the experience you just had and how you feel about it.

AFTER WRITING

Read this piece of writing out loud to yourself. Notice how you approached this person to ask for something. Were you able to ask for what you needed directly, with dignity and respect? Or did you have to beat around the bush or imply your request? Did you feel you had to apologize for asking? (For example, did you say something like, "Listen, I feel really bad about this, I'm really a jerk and I know I don't deserve it, but do you think maybe, if I promise to pay you back with fifty-percent interest, by next Tuesday, do you think you can lend me five bucks?")

Notice how you respond when someone says yes and when someone says no. If they say yes, are you surprised? Do you fall all over yourself to thank them? If they say no, do you feel bad for asking? Do you try to get them to change their mind? Or did you know all along that they'd say no, so why bother anyway?

DISCUSSION AND HOMEWORK

At least once a day for a week, ask someone for something you want or need. For example, you can ask a friend for a hug, ask someone to take a walk with you, or to go to the movies with you, ask someone for a backrub or a ride to work or to help you tune up your bike or to lend you their sewing machine. Notice how you feel before you ask, while you are asking, and after you ask. Notice how you respond when someone says yes and when someone says no. If you ask for something you need seven days in a row, chances are you will experience both responses.

When someone says yes, can you take that in, or do you feel bad for asking? When someone says no, can you accept that her reasoning has to do with her own limits, or do you take it personally? If you

ask someone to give you a back rub and she says
no because she has to pick up her daughter from
childcare in fifteen minutes, that doesn't mean you
are a bad person for asking, or that you should feel
guilty, or even that you need to offer to pick up her
child. It simply means that you and she had
different needs at that time. That's it. Period.
There's no one to blame. You may feel angry, hurt,
or rejected, and that's fine. Those are your feelings.
They have little to do with your friend. They have
to do with you. Notice your feelings and accept
them. Try not to judge yourself for having them.

SAYING NO

This exercise can be done either as a writing exercise or out loud with a friend. If you are doing it with a friend, have her ask you to borrow something—the watch you're wearing, or a bracelet or a ring. You are not to let her have it. Have her keep asking you. Keep saying no. Even if you don't want to. Do this for five minutes. Then take ten minutes to write about how you felt while you were saying no. Write without stopping.

If you are doing this exercise alone, imagine a friend of yours asking you to borrow something—your favorite sweater for example, or a piece of jewelry you especially like. Let yourself say no to her. Imagine her asking you at least ten times. You job is to keep saying no, no matter what. Then take ten minutes to describe this experience and how you felt about it. Write without stopping.

AFTER WRITING

Read what you wrote out loud. Did you feel guilty for saying no? Did you feel you had to have an excuse? That the whole thing is silly, why not just let her have it? Did you get angry? Did you feel powerful? Did you wish she would just stop asking you already? Were you able to keep saying no, or did you give in?

Whatever you did was the right thing for you to do. If you gave in, you did not "fail" this exercise. I

will not give you an F. However you responded is
important information for you to have about
yourself.

Many women with eating dis-eases find it
especially hard to say no. We feel like we have to
please everyone—our parents, our friends, our lover,
our children, the mail carrier, strangers on the
street—everyone but ourselves. When we say yes to
someone without really wanting to, what we are
really doing is saying no to ourselves. Why is it so
easy for you to say no to yourself, but so hard to
say no to anybody else?

It is hard to remember that your needs are just as
important as everyone else's. It is okay to say no.
Many of us were told we were selfish for saying no.
I think being self-ish is very healthy. Looking after
yourself, and giving yourself what you need are
ways of loving yourself. So is saying no to
something you don't want to do.

Think of it this way: when you say no to
someone else, you are actually doing them a favor. I
know, I know, you don't believe me. You want me
to prove it. Okay. Let's say someone calls you up
and asks if she can tell you about a problem she's
having because she needs some advice. You say yes,
but you really want to say no because you have to
leave the house in five minutes to get to a doctor's
appointment. You were afraid if you said no, your
friend would get mad at you. So while she is
talking, you are putting on your shoes, searching
for your car keys, trying to remember how to get to
the doctor's, and wishing that your friend would
hurry up and finish talking. Does this sound
familiar? You are not helping your friend at all,
even though you said yes. Au contraire, my dear. In
this situation, if you say no, your friend has several
choices. She can call someone else who is more

available at that moment, she can call you back later, she can write about it in her journal, or she can let go of it for a while. She won't die. She will probably still be your friend. And you'll get what you need too, which is to get off the phone, out of the house, and to your appointment.

HOMEWORK

Say no at least once a day for a week. You don't have to make any excuses or give long-winded explanations, or even apologize. If you feel really uncomfortable, you can say, "Well, I'm reading this very bizarre book, and my homework is to say no, so I'm saying no." If someone has to take the blame, I will. But really, just try to say no. You can do it in a loving way—loving to yourself and loving to the person who's asking you for something. Write about the different experiences you have and how you feel about them.

MOTHERS

Imagine your mother eating a meal. Notice where
she is eating. Is she at a fancy restaurant, sitting at
the kitchen table, standing at the stove, in front of
the TV? Picture what she is wearing and how she
holds her body. Does your mother eat quickly or
slowly? Does she enjoy her food? Does she satisfy
her appetite, or does she eat less than she really
wants? Does she overeat? If she is eating with other
people, how does her food differ from theirs? How
does she interact with those around her? If she is
eating alone, does she engage in other activities
while she eats? How does she feel about the food
she is eating? Take twenty minutes to describe, in as
much detail as possible, your mother eating a meal.
Write without stopping.

AFTER WRITING

Read this piece of writing out loud to yourself.
Notice the messages, both verbal and non-verbal,
that you received from your mother about being a
woman in a woman's body, about women and food,
about women and pleasure. Note how these
messages were communicated. For example,
suppose you wrote, "My mother always served my
father and three brothers first. Then she ate while
standing at the stove, waiting to serve them
seconds." The implied message here is that women's
appetites are second to men's. If you wrote, "My
mother stared at the chocolate cake wistfully and

said, 'I'd really like a piece but I have to watch my weight,'" the message you received was that women are not allowed to give themselves what they want. There is too high a price to pay. In this case, this particular women will not allow herself the pleasure of eating something delicious for fear that she will "pay the price" of gaining weight. Suppose you wrote, "My mother cut herself a wedge of apple pie and ate it with great enthusiasm. Then she put the pie away so she could have the rest tomorrow." The message you received was that women are allowed to give themselves pleasure, even two days in a row!

Re-read what you wrote and make a list of all the messages, both silent and spoken that you received from your mother about women, eating, and food.

HOMEWORK

Mother/daughter relationships are very complicated. Your mother was the first woman you ever loved, and whether you like it or not, she had a tremendous impact on your life. Keeping in mind the new information you have gleaned from the writing exercise, write your mother a letter (that you may or may not send to her) in which you tell her how you feel about growing up with the messages she gave you about being a woman in a woman's body. Be honest. You do not have to show her or anybody else this letter. You are writing it for you. Let yourself be angry, sad, lonely, proud, happy, defiant, vengeful, enraged, or however else you feel.

If you are thinking about mailing this letter to your mother, let it sit for at least a week before you make that decision. You may or may not want to read it to a friend or a therapist as part of your decision-making process. Whatever you decide is the right decision for you. If you choose to send your letter, and your mother responds in a way that does not please you, that doesn't mean you made the wrong decision. You cannot control other people. You did what you needed to do for you.

FANTASY MOTHERS

Picture yourself as a little girl, crying. Perhaps you fell down and hurt yourself, or the boy next door grabbed your favorite stuffed animal and threw her down the sewer. Maybe you want something you can't have, or maybe you're just plain tired. If you can't actually remember yourself crying, try to imagine it.

Now imagine a woman coming to comfort you. This is your fantasy mother. She may or may not resemble your actual mother. Notice now she cares for you, pays attention to you and soothes you. Let her give you exactly what you need—even if you think your needs are too big, or that you don't deserve it. Your fantasy mother has all the time in the world, all the money in the world, all the love in the world, everything that could possibly be needed to take care of you.

Take twenty minutes to describe this experience and how you feel about it. Write without stopping.

AFTER WRITING

The purpose of this exercise is not to blame your mother for not being perfect. Your mother did the best she could. She had her own needs to worry about, as well as yours. Chances are good that she wasn't taught how to take care of herself and to take care of a child as well. I'm sure she made mistakes, as all human beings do. That doesn't mean you should or shouldn't feel angry at her. Whatever feelings you have about your mother are fine.

The wonderful thing about your fantasy mother is that she has no needs of her own. She is there just for you. Read what you've written out loud to yourself. Notice now you felt when your fantasy mother took care of you. Were you happy, sad, distrustful, embarrassed? Were you able to let her comfort you? It's okay if you could not let her close to you. Often it is hard to let someone else take care of us if we're not used to it. Sometimes a woman will feel sad when someone finally pays attention to her needs, because then she remembers all the times her needs weren't attended to. However you respond to your fantasy mother is fine.

HOMEWORK

Write a letter from your fantasy mother to yourself every day for a week, in which she tells you how wonderful you are. Remember your fantasy mother has been created just for you. Let her love you unconditionally. Think about how everyone loves a newborn baby, just for existing in the world. That's how your fantasy mother feels about you.

FATHERS

Picture yourself standing next to your father when you were a little girl. Your father is describing you. He may be talking to a specific person, or he may be addressing no one in particular. What tone of voice does he use? What words does he choose to describe how you look, what you do, and how he feels about you? Imagine yourself getting older. Now you are a teenager. How does your father describe you at this age? Is he proud of you, ashamed of you, angry at you? Does he feel differently than when you were a little girl? Now picture yourself as you are today, standing next to your father. How does he describe this woman who is his daughter? How does he feel about the choices you've made in your life?

Take twenty minutes to write, in your father's voice, descriptions of you at these three different ages. Start with the words "This is my daughter _____" (your name). Write without stopping.

AFTER WRITING

Read what you've written out loud to yourself. Notice the messages, both verbal and non-verbal your father gave to you. Was he consistently proud of you as you grew up, or was he ashamed of you? Or did he give you mixed messages? How did this affect you? Were you always trying to please him, or did you rebel against him?

Notice in particular what your father said about your appearance. If you wrote (in your father's voice), "This is my daughter Rachel. She has a pretty face, but she could stand to lose a few pounds," how did that affect your self esteem? If you wrote, "This is my daughter Becky. Doesn't she look adorable in her new blue overalls?" how did you feel about yourself? Make a list of all the messages, both spoken and implied that your father communicated about how he felt toward you and your body.

DISCUSSION AND HOMEWORK

The messages we receive from our parents affect us very powerfully. If your father said to you one day, "You really could stand to lose some weight," chances are he forgot about it within the hour. You, on the other hand, may still be carrying that message around five, ten, thirty-five years later.

Write a letter to your father telling him exactly how you feel about all the messages he gave you about your body, mind, and spirit as you were growing up. Give yourself permission to feel angry, sad, proud, happy, enraged, depressed, defiant, vengeful, or to have any other emotions. Remember this letter is for you. You may or may not send it.

We women with eating dis-eases often have trouble feeling our feelings, because we think we shouldn't feel a certain way, and it's hard to accept that we in fact do feel that way. It is fine, for example, if you feel that you love your father more than your mother because he spoiled you rotten, and your mother didn't always let you have your way. Or you may hate your father because every single day of your childhood and adolescence he made derogatory comments about your body. He (or other male authority figures) may also have made you feel bad about your body without words, with a look or an unwanted touch. Many of us have been abused emotionally and/or sexually by family members, leaving us, among other things, confused about our feelings toward them. Often we love them and hate them at the same time.

Feelings are not actions. It is okay to hate someone so much that you want to kill them, but it is not okay to kill them. Feelings pass, actions do not. If you hate your father or your mother, or anyone else, and you let yourself express it, chances are you will let go of it a lot faster, though that is not necessarily your goal. More importantly, expressing yourself will help you avoid turning that hatred onto yourself and acting out in destructive ways with food.

If you are considering mailing your letter to your father, let it sit for a week before you decide what to do. You may or may not want to read it to a friend or therapist as part of your decision-making process. Whatever you decide is the right decision for you. If you choose to send your letter and your father responds in a way that does not please you, that doesn't mean you made the wrong decision. You can't control other people. You did what you needed to do, for yourself.

FAMILIES

Now that we've worked with mothers and fathers, let's bring out the rest of the family. Imagine a typical dinner scene from your adolescence. Who else ate with you besides your parents? Brothers, sisters, grandparents, cousins, pets? Imagine the room in which you sat—and see all the people around the table. Take your time and notice what everyone is eating. How is the food served? Are bowls and platters passed around, or is each person served individually by one of the adults? Are people talking to each other? If so, what is the content of the conversation? How are seconds handled? thirds? dessert? Do people leave the table when they are through, or do they wait to be excused? Who clears off the table and who washes the dishes?

Take twenty minutes to describe this scene, in as much detail as possible, *writing from the point of view of an inanimate object on the table*—the salt shaker for example, or the napkin holder. Write in first person and write without stopping. This is the idea: "I am the salt shaker, standing at attention on the Newman family's dinner table. To my left is a little girl named Lesléa. She looks very sad. When her mother turns her back, she feeds little bits of meat to her dog, who is sitting under her chair. Across the table from Lesléa is her father. He is sopping up gravy with a piece of Wonderbread...." Got it? Go.

AFTER WRITING

Read this piece of writing out loud to yourself. Suppose you were reading a scene like this and it was not your family, so that you could look at the situation objectively. Observing this scene as if you were watching a scene from a play, what observations would you make? What is the overall atmosphere of the meal? Are the characters relaxed, nervous, tense, eager? Is the conversation confrontive, loving, cold? How are the characters relating to one another? Does each one take equal part in the conversation? Does one character dominate? Does one character fade into the background silently? Are there characters who have major conflicts with each other? Is there a power struggle going on? Do the characters focus on the food? Do they enjoy what they're eating? Who has control over what goes on everyone's plate? Do the characters comment on the food, or on what each person is eating? Make a list of your observations. This is very important information.

DISCUSSION AND HOMEWORK

Dinnertime is often the only time all of the members of a family get together, so it is sometimes quite stressful. It is important to make dinner a nurturing experience for yourself. Dinner comes at the end of your day, after working, going to school, or participating in other activities that may have been stressful. It is the gateway into evening and night, which also may contain stressful situations—work, school, new social settings. If dinner was not a relaxing event when you were growing up, chances are that you may be continuing that pattern, either by eating on the run, engaging in other activities while eating, bringing up issues that involve conflict during dinner, or skipping the meal altogether.

At least two times this week, have dinner with people you consider "family" and make the event nourishing, both physically and emotionally. People in your "family" can include good friends, lovers, spouses, children, neighbors, or people from your family of origin. Think about what would nourish you—a picnic, going out to a restaurant, a home-cooked meal at someone else's house or at home. Let yourself really enjoy these meals. An enjoyable dinner is good preventative medicine, especially for late-night bingers. If you give yourself what you want, and let yourself feel satisfied, chances are you will be less inclined to hurt yourself later in the night with food.

EATING ALONE

Imagine yourself eating dinner alone, at home.
Watch yourself prepare the food—taking it out of
the refrigerator or cupboard, or going out to the
store and buying it. Watch yourself cut, chop, slice,
fry, saute, bake, or simply unwrap what you have
chosen for yourself. Now watch yourself eat. Notice
where you are sitting or standing, and how you eat
your food. What are you feeling as you eat this
meal? What are you thinking about? Are you
enjoying your food? What do you do when the
meal is over? Do you have seconds? dessert? Do
you wash your dishes right away? How do you feel
when the meal is over? Take twenty minutes to
describe, in as much detail as possible, what you
just experienced and how you feel about it. Write
without stopping.

AFTER WRITING

Read this piece of writing out loud to yourself.
How did you go about choosing the food that you
ate? Did you think about what you wanted and let
yourself have it, or did you eat what you thought
you should? Did you think about calories and
carbohydrates? Were you happy with your
selection? Were you looking forward to this meal or
dreading it?

Did you take the time to prepare your food in a
loving way, or did you just throw something
together? Did you set the table for yourself, or did

you eat standing up? Did you do other things while
you ate, such as read, watch TV, talk on the phone,
fix the radio, make a list of everything you have to
do tomorrow? After you ate did you feel satisfied?
Did you wish you'd eaten less? Did you want to eat
more? Were you sad that the meal was over? Or
were you relieved?

DISCUSSION AND HOMEWORK

Many women feel if they eat alone it's not worth
the trouble to cook something special, just for
themselves. Peanut butter on crackers, leftover cold
pizza, any old thing will do. I disagree. If you don't
think you're special and worth making a fuss over,
not many other people will think so either. You
deserve to treat yourself as though you were your
most favorite person in the world. You are going to
spend the rest of your life with you. You might as
well learn to love yourself, your very own constant
companion.

   At least three times this week, eat dinner alone
and make it a special treat for yourself. Even if you
have a family that you need to attend to first. Even
if you live in a cooperative household where you all
work and eat together. This will give you good
practice in asking for what you need, and you
definitely need the people around you to support
you in your healing process.

   Court yourself as you would a lover. Woo
yourself with your favorite foods, candlelight,
flowers. You are worth this special attention. If you
can't have privacy in your kitchen or dining room,
set up a space for yourself in your bedroom. If that
isn't feasible, take yourself out to dinner, or ask a
friend who lives alone if you can use her apartment.

Set the table with the bowls, plates, cups, glasses, silverware or chopsticks you especially like. Sit down and leisurely enjoy your meal. Try not to distract yourself by reading, watching TV, or doing any other activity. If the phone rings, let someone else get it. If it's for you, have someone take a message. I personally think answering machines are the greatest invention since matzo ball soup. I always turn my machine on during dinner. Again, this is putting out your needs. If someone calls while I'm eating, they can wait fifteen minutes for me to call them back. If I talk on the phone while I'm eating, I can't concentrate on the meal or on the conversation, and I usually get a crook in my neck, spill something on my sweater, and get the phone all greasy. If I interrupt my dinner, my food gets cold (have you ever tried to eat cold matzo ball soup?) and I get grumpy.

It's the same thing if you eat and read, a common activity among women with eating dis-eases. It's hard to concentrate on what you're reading or on what you're eating and if you're a bit of a klutz like me, you wind up getting spaghetti sauce on the pages and the librarian gets angry.

Make dinner alone a sensual experience for yourself, like taking an herbal bath by candlelight. Give yourself the gift of deriving pleasure from a meal. You would make a fuss over someone you really care about, wouldn't you? Let that someone be yourself.

INTIMATE RELATIONSHIPS

Imagine yourself eating a meal with a lover, either someone you are currently involved with, or someone you have been involved with. If you have never had a lover, imagine sharing a meal with someone you are attracted to. Notice where you are eating—in a home, in a restaurant, on the beach. Notice what you are eating and what your lover is eating. Do you eat the same foods? The same amount of food? How do you feel about the food on your plate, and about the food on your lover's plate? Be aware of your body during this meal. How do you hold yourself? Are you comfortable or tense? How do you feel about your lover's body? Do you touch while you eat? Do you talk? Do you look at each other? What happens when the meal is over? Take twenty minutes to describe this meal in as much detail as possible and how you feel about it. Write without stopping.

AFTER WRITING

Read what you've written out loud to yourself. Was this a pleasurable experience for you? Did you let yourself eat what you wanted in front of your lover? Or did you eat what you thought you should? Did you try to impress your lover by eating only a little (being "good" by sticking to your diet)? If your lover ate more than you, or different foods than you, did you feel angry, jealous, superior, indifferent? If your lover ate less than you, did you feel embarrassed, guilty, angry, indifferent? Were you comfortable in your body during this meal? Did you stand, sit, or lie down so that you would look as thin as possible? Did you try to hide different parts of your body? How did your lover hold her or his body during this meal? How did you feel about your lover's body? How much attention did you pay to the food and to your lover? If your lover is smaller than you, are you jealous? If your lover is larger than you, are you smug? Did you feel at ease with your lover? If you felt nervous or tense, were you able to deal with these feelings, or did you overeat/undereat to avoid them? Did the calorie counter in your brain start ticking away at the first sign of tension (sexual or otherwise)? Make a list of everything you observed about this meal.

DISCUSSION AND HOMEWORK

If you haven't guessed by now, your homework is to share a meal with a lover or someone you are attracted to. If you are not currently involved with someone, see if you can ask someone out on a date. You are a sexual being with sexual feelings, no matter what you weigh, and you deserve to explore that part of yourself. You don't have to have sex with this person. Just dinner. The person you ask will probably be very flattered, whether it's someone you're asking out for the first time, or the person you've been involved with for twenty-five years. If the person you ask says no, remember that their response has more to do with them than it does with you. It does not mean there is anything wrong with you, or that it was wrong of you to ask. See if you can ask someone else.

Make this dinner a pleasurable experience for yourself. Choose a restaurant you enjoy, or cook foods you especially like. Dress in comfortable clothing that you feel attractive in. If, during this meal, negative thoughts come into your mind (for example, "I shouldn't be eating this much," or "so-and-so probably thinks I'm a jerk"), let those thoughts go. Concentrate instead on what is happening in the moment—"I am chewing a piece of lasagna," "I am holding so-and-so's hand," "The waitperson is telling me tonight's specials." Try and stay in the moment as much as possible. Have a great time.

SEXUALITY AND BODY SIZE

Imagine yourself having dinner with your current/former/potential lover once more. Set the scene in your mind, so that it is a nourishing situation for you. Now imagine that someone waves a magic wand and you've suddenly gained 100 pounds. How does the scene change? Are you now wearing different clothes?

Are you now eating different foods or amounts of food? How do you feel about yourself in this new body? Do you feel differently toward your lover? How do you interact with your lover? Do you touch, make eye contact, talk with each other?

Now imagine that the magic wand is waved again, and all of a sudden you are very very thin. How does the scene change? Are you wearing different clothes? Are you now eating different foods or different amounts of food? How do you feel about yourself in this new body? Do you feel differently toward your lover? How do you interact with your lover? Do you touch, make eye contact, talk with each other?

For the third and last time, the magic wand is waved over your head. Now you are back to your actual size, the size you are right now. How do you feel about being in this body? How do you interact with your lover now?

Take twenty minutes to describe this experience and how you feel about it. Write in as much detail as possible and write without stopping.

AFTER WRITING

Read what you wrote out loud to yourself. Notice the different ways you felt in your different bodies. When you were 100 pounds heavier, did you wear clothing that would hide or show your body? Did you eat more or less in front of your lover? Were you shy, uncomfortable, more relaxed than usual? Did you feel sexual? Were you more or less affectionate and flirtatious with your lover? Did you have feelings of jealousy or anger because your lover's body was smaller than yours? Did you think your lover wouldn't want to be sexual with you because you were 100 pounds heavier? If so, how did you feel about that—angry, depressed, relieved?

When you became thin, did you eat more or less? Did you wear clothes that would hide or show your body? Were you more or less affectionate and flirtatious with your lover? Were you shy, uncomfortable, more relaxed? Did you feel sexual? Did you have feelings of fear, anger, or jealousy because your lover's body was bigger than yours? Did you think your lover wouldn't want to be sexual with you because you were thin? If so, how did you feel about that—angry, depressed, relieved?

When you returned to your actual body size, were you relieved or did you wish you could stay either heavier, or very thin? Did you have a new perspective on your body, after having imagined it transformed? Write down all your observations about your feelings about these different body sizes.

DISCUSSION AND HOMEWORK

Many women have mixed feelings about being fat and being thin, and a lot of those feelings have to do with sexuality. Many of us have had unpleasant and even violent sexual experiences such as incest, rape, date rape, and marital rape. Diana Russell reports that 38 percent of a random sample of 930 women reported they had been sexually abused before the age of 18.*

I firmly believe that sexual abuse and eating dis-eases are directly related. When someone hurts our bodies, we often hate our bodies instead of our abusers. One woman in one of my workshops told how she came home from playing in the park one day, crying because some boys had pinched her nipples (she was about eleven years old). Her mother scolded her for wearing a tank top and took her out to buy her first bra on the spot. From that day on she hated her breasts. She then became anorexic as a way to stop her breasts from developing.

Many women can trace the onset of their eating dis-ease as a response to sexual abuse, though they didn't know it at the time. Some women begin to binge and put on weight, buying into the myth that fat women are not sexually attractive—a false statement that our culture tries to teach us. Other women begin to starve themselves as an attempt to make their hips, thighs, breasts, and belly disappear, so they can retreat back into a little girl's body, where they feel safer.

It is important to look at your own attitude toward your body and your sexuality. Make a list of the important sexual experiences in your life, and what size your body was during those times. Do you see some kind of pattern emerging? Do you use

---

*   *The Secret Trauma* (New York: Basic Books, 1986).

being fat or being thin as a way to say no to
unwanted sexual advances? Do you change your
body size to avoid or invite certain kinds of
situations?

Sexual experiences, both good and bad, have
profound effects on all of us. If while writing about
your sexuality you uncover some unpleasant or
painful memories, find a safe place to talk about
them. I suggest a therapist, a trusted friend, Incest
Survivors Anonymous (a free, twelve-step recovery
program), or the hotline of a local women's center
or shelter. Even if your abuse happened 35 years
ago, and you think, "It's no big deal. I don't need
to talk about it," I urge you to make that phone
call anyway. Sexual abuse is always a big deal. If it
happened to a child or a woman you cared about,
you would urge her to take care of herself, I'm sure.
Please be as loving and caring to yourself.

MAKING LOVE

Think about the last time you made love with someone. Close your eyes and picture the scene. Were you in a bedroom, in a tent, on top of a mountain? Was it daytime or night? Was there music or silence, candlelight or darkness? Were you on a bed, on the floor, in the grass, on a chair?

Watch yourself with your lover. How do you feel about your body? How do you feel about your lover's body? Is this a pleasurable experience for you? Are you getting what you need? How do you feel while making love? How do you feel afterward? Do you communicate your needs to your lover, or do you keep them inside yourself? Take twenty minutes to describe this experience and how you feel about it. Write without stopping.

AFTER WRITING

Read this piece of writing out loud to yourself. How do you feel about your sexual activity? When you visualized yourself making love were you happy, fearful, ashamed, sad, angry? Did you feel pleasure, or were you uptight? Were you anxious about performing? Were you more concerned with pleasing your lover than pleasing yourself? Did you feel comfortable with this person? Did you feel good about your body? Did you feel sexy and attractive, or ugly? Did you find your lover attractive? Were you able to ask your lover for what you need, or did you hope he or she would guess? How did you feel after you made love? Were you happy, sad, ashamed, scared, angry, proud, depressed? Did you feel close to your lover? Did you want to snuggle or be alone, have sex again, eat? Are you able to talk about your feelings with your lover?

DISCUSSION AND HOMEWORK

Many women with eating dis-eases have a lot of issues around sexuality. We are so vulnerable when we are naked in front of someone else—when we admit that we exist from the neck down and that we have sexual desires. What if our lover rejects us, or finds us ugly? So often we find ourselves ugly that we project this onto our lovers—if they love us, stupid, ugly us, there must be something wrong with them. Couldn't they find anyone better? What's their problem? Or, we'll do one of my all-time favorites—we'll ask our lover (often in the most intimate moment) "Honey, do you think I'm too fat?" (Does this sound familiar?)

This question has no right answer. If your lover says, "No Sweetheart, I think you're beautiful just the way you are," you won't believe it for a minute (if you believed it you wouldn't have had to ask). If your lover says, "Well, to tell you the truth, you could lose five pounds," you'll think, "I knew it. Even my lover thinks I'm unattractive. I'm worthless."

Asking this question is a perfect set-up to make you feel lousy.

For homework, have a positive sexual experience with yourself. Masturbation is a wonderful way to get to know your body, to heal yourself, and to learn what gives you pleasure. Give yourself at least an hour for this exercise. Make sure you won't be interrupted.

Prepare yourself just as you would for a lover. Take a bath, oil your skin, bring candles and flowers into your room, make the bed with satin sheets. Use this time to explore every inch of your body. Treat yourself lovingly. You know better than anyone else what feels good to you and what doesn't. If you don't know, now is a good time to find out. If you have negative thoughts about your body during this experience ("Ugh, that layer of fat around my hips is disgusting," or "I hate the bulge around my belly"), disrupt those thoughts by focusing on the moment. Say out loud to yourself, "My hand is on my hip," or "I am touching my belly." These statements carry no judgments. Stay present, let thoughts go in and out of your mind and let yourself feel.

Make friends with your body by touching it in new ways as well as in old familiar ways. You won't be able to tell your lover what feels good if you don't know yourself. The more relaxed you can be with yourself, the more comfortable you can be with a partner. Alone you don't have to suck in your stomach or stay lying on your back so your belly looks flat, or raise your arms over your head so your rib cage will be more pronounced. Alone you don't have to make love in the dark or hide your body under the sheets so your lover won't see your stretch marks. The more comfortable you are with your body, the more comfortable you will be able to be with someone else. Take your time both during and after this exercise. You probably wouldn't jump up and race to the grocery store after making love with someone else, would you? You deserve the same treatment. Luxuriate in your

own sensuality and sexuality. If this seems
indulgent, it is. Indulge yourself in your own
pleasure. You deserve it. Take some time to write
about this experience.

FAT WOMEN AND THIN WOMEN

You are now going to create two characters who you will then write about. To do this, answer the following questions about each of them. You don't have to base these characters on anyone you know—you will be making them up as you go along. Your characters can be whoever you want them to be. They can be nice or nasty, loveable or despicable. Be creative and have fun!

The first character you will be creating is a fat woman.

Name: _____

Age: _____

Physical appearance

  Height: _____

  Weight: _____

  Hair color and style: _____

  Facial features: _____

  Distinguishing marks or scars: _____

  What is she wearing: _____

Job: _____

Hobbies: _____

Housing: _____

Expressions she uses frequently: _____

Annoying habits: _____

Pet peeves: _____

Biggest fear: _____

Secret desire: _____

What she is most proud of: _____

What she is most ashamed of: _____
Favorite food: _____
Favorite color: _____
Favorite music: _____
Magazines she subscribes to: _____
Book she is currently reading: _____
Typical meal: _____
Typical Saturday night: _____
Significant others (friends/lovers): _____
Pets: _____
Mode of transportation: _____
Family background: _____

Now answer the same questions for your second character, who is a thin woman:

Name: _____
Age: _____
Physical appearance
  Height: _____
  Weight: _____
  Hair color and style: _____
  Facial features: _____
  Distinguishing marks or scars: _____
  What is she wearing: _____
Job: _____
Hobbies: _____
Housing: _____
Expressions she uses frequently: _____
Annoying habits: _____
Pet peeves: _____
Biggest fear: _____
Secret desire: _____
What she is most proud of: _____
What she is most ashamed of: _____
Favorite food: _____

Favorite color: _____

Favorite music: _____

Magazines she subscribes to: _____

Book she is currently reading: _____

Typical meal: _____

Typical Saturday night: _____

Significant others (friends/lovers): _____

Pets: _____

Mode of transportation: _____

Family background: _____

These two women are going to eat a meal together. Take twenty minutes to write the scene and the conversation. Write without stopping and describe what the women eat and how they interact with each other. Don't spend too much time getting them to the table (or to the beach, or to wherever it is they're eating). Somehow they have met and made this date to share a meal together. Take it from there.

AFTER WRITING

Read what you have written out loud to yourself. If you can, find two friends who will read this piece of writing out loud, each one taking the part of one woman. What observations can you make? Does the fat woman eat less than the thin woman, or vice versa? Who seems to be more outgoing and confident, more comfortable with herself? Who is a better listener? Who talks more about herself? Which of the two women seems happy with her life? Who has a satisfying job, good friends, a meaningful intimate relationship? Which woman enjoys her food? Which woman is at ease with her body? Who dresses in an attractive manner? Who has a sense of humor?

Is the thin woman thin because she's on a diet, or because she's just built that way? Is the fat woman fat because she binges, or because she is built that way? Which woman do you identify with? Who would you like to be? Your answer may surprise you. Make a list of your observations about these two women and how you relate to them.

DISCUSSION AND HOMEWORK

I have done this exercise with different groups of women many times over the past eight years. When I first started doing it, I was very surprised that the group made the thin woman very nasty, bitter, and unhappy with her life, even though she usually had the right "trappings": a few boyfriends, great clothes, nice apartment, high-paying job. On the other hand, the fat woman is usually portrayed as happy, enjoying life, optimistic, and interested in her companion, though her material possessions are few and she usually doesn't have a lover (more often she has a cat). The fat woman is usually on some kind of diet, though not sticking to it, and the thin woman usually exists on cottage cheese and carrot sticks. (If your characters are different than what I've just described that's fine. It doesn't mean you did anything wrong.)

What I've concluded about this is that the thin woman is unhappy because she is constantly depriving herself in order to maintain the "right" appearance. The fat woman is happier because she allows herself pleasure. There is more to each of these characters than meets the eye. Take each of them separately and write a letter in her voice, addressed to you, starting with the sentence, "This is what I could never tell you." Write in each character's voice for fifteen minutes without stopping. You may be surprised at the secrets these characters hold for you.

ANGER

Take ten minutes to make a list of all the people who have ever made a negative remark about your body. Include (if appropriate) family members, peers, authority figures, lovers, health care workers, children, strangers, etc.

Pick one of the people on the list, preferably the one you feel the most anger toward. If you are not in touch with feelings of anger, pick the first person who comes to mind, or choose someone at random. Think back to the actual incident. How were you interacting with this person? What were you wearing? What did he or she say to you exactly? How did you feel? What did you do?

Write a letter to this person, telling him or her just how you feel about what happened. Remember this letter is for you. You don't have to send it. No one else ever has to see it. Say whatever it is that you need to say. Write for fifteen minutes without stopping.

AFTER WRITING

Read this letter out loud to yourself. What is the tone of the letter—angry, sad, bitter, depressed, dejected, proud? Did you feel you had to protect the person who insulted you, either by taking care of them, making excuses for them, or forgiving them? Did you think deep down that they were right? Did you get angry at the person who violated you, or did you get angry at yourself? Did your relationship with this person change after this incident? Did you feel differently toward your own body afterward? Did your eating habits change?

DISCUSSION AND HOMEWORK

As women, we are well trained to be "nice." Many traditional women's jobs list "pleasant personality" as one of their criteria. Can you imagine a traditional man's job, such as a truck driver, construction worker, or bank president, requiring a pleasant personality? Women who are assertive and direct are usually labeled "bitchy." We are taught to swallow our anger, and many women with eating dis-eases literally stuff down their rage with food. Often we don't even get angry when someone is downright mean to us. Instead we make excuses: "Oh, he's just having a bad day" or "Maybe you're right. This outfit" (on which you just spent half your paycheck) "does make me look terrible. I know you're telling me for my own good. Thank you."

I think feeling angry is a healthy way to respond when someone hurts us. Being angry means I feel like a worthwhile person. No one has the right to abuse me. By taking on someone else's anger and getting depressed, or becoming self-abusive, I am giving myself the message that I really don't deserve to take up any space on the planet.

Most of the people on your list probably don't even remember the comments they made about your body. Yet they have been affecting *your* life for five, ten, thirty, fifty years! How do you feel about that? Work your way down your list, and write a letter to each and every one of these people telling them how you feel about what they said to you. It is okay to

get angry, even at people you love. You have
probably underestimated the amount of damage
done to the little girl inside of you, every time
someone verbally abused your body. Let your
feelings out in these letters. You may or may not
decide to send some of these letters, or to let some
of these people know how you feel, by calling them
or talking with them face to face. If you do choose
to confront someone, try to keep the focus on
yourself. Instead of saying, "You were such a jerk
when you said . . .," try to rephrase your statement:
"I felt so _____ (angry, hurt, devastated, or
whatever) when you said . . ." Being angry doesn't
give anyone—including you—the right to become
verbally abusive. If you express your feelings by
keeping the focus on yourself and refraining from
attacking the person you are talking to, you will
create a safe situation for open communication. If
the person you are talking to doesn't feel attacked,
he or she won't have to get defensive or attack back.

Direct communication is different than writing
letters you know you will never send. If you want
to call someone a jerk, an idiot, or an insensitive
creep, a letter is a good place to do it. Read that
letter to a friend, or rip it up, or burn it. We all feel
that angry at someone sometimes. I have never
found insulting someone directly very helpful,
though I may sometimes need to rage at them
privately or on paper. Punching pillows isn't such a
bad idea either. Or screaming in your car. Every
woman has anger inside her. You are not bad when
you feel angry. Expressing anger in constructive
ways is very healing. Try it.

RESCUING THE LITTLE GIRL WITHIN

Imagine yourself as a little girl, a child who is basically happy, who likes to play and laugh and explore the world. If you can't remember such a time in your life, try to imagine it anyway. All of us are born feeling good about ourselves. This good feeling may have been taken away from you when you were one hour old, but still there was a time when you had it.

Imagine someone from the list you compiled of people who made negative comments about your body approaching this child and verbally abusing her. How does the child respond? Now, imagine yourself as the adult you are today, stepping in and interrupting the situation. Watch yourself make an intervention and rescue the little girl. How do you make her feel safe? Can you ask her what she needs? Can you give her what she needs?

Take as much time as is necessary to comfort that little girl in the way you would have wanted to be comforted when this type of thing happened to you. Then take fifteen minutes to write about this experience and how you feel about it. Write without stopping.

AFTER WRITING

Read this piece of writing out loud to yourself. How did you feel watching the little girl inside you going through this situation? Did you feel sad, angry, annoyed, apathetic, frustrated, depressed or enraged? Did you feel foolish imagining that there is a little girl inside you at all? Were you able to watch yourself as an adult rescue yourself as a child?

What did the child need from you—a hug, a new teddy bear, a story? Were you able to give her what she needed? How did you feel comforting her—happy, scared, angry, annoyed, satisfied, compassionate, foolish, impatient, tender? Were you able to pay full attention to her, or were you concerned with taking care of the person who hurt her as well? Is she at a place now where she feels safe? Write down your observations.

DISCUSSION AND HOMEWORK

All of us are born loving ourselves, and the minute someone hurts us by telling us there is something wrong with the way we look, most of us change from being a joyful little girl full of self-love into a sad little girl full of self-hate, no matter how old we were when the abuse happened. If an adult steps in and takes care of the little girl in appropriate ways (by telling her she's not too fat, she's perfect and beautiful just the way she is), the healing starts to happen immediately. If no intervention takes place, or even worse, if an adult steps in and supports the abuser (saying "Yeah, why don't you lose some weight? You'd look a lot better."), more hurt gets piled onto the original hurt, and the sad little girl full of self-hate gets even sadder and more full of self-hate.

Over the next few weeks, go down your list of people who made negative comments about your body and replay the situation in your mind. Envision yourself stepping in as an adult and disrupting the abuse. Let your adult take care of the little girl inside you, in exactly the way she wants to be taken care of. If this is difficult for you, imagine someone you love in the same situation—your child, your best friend, your lover. Would you have an easier time rescuing them? You deserve the same protection, love, and care.

Have the little girl inside you write the adult you a letter every day for a week, in which she tells you what she wants. Often, to get in touch with her, it is helpful to write with the hand you ordinarily don't write with (if you're a lefty, use your right hand, if you're a righty, use your left). See if you can give that little girl what she needs. (I myself bought my first teddy bear at age 27; her name is Bartleby.)

Many women with eating dis-eases find using a pacifier or drinking juice out of a bottle helpful. Many of us never learned how to play; we were too busy trying to be perfect. Coloring books and crayons, finger paints, jump rope, jacks, Matchbox cars and Slinkys are all great. Maybe a friend would read you a story and tuck you in one night. The more you take care of that little girl, the less likely she'll appear at inappropriate moments (like at a staff meeting), making unreasonable demands (can we go home now?). As the button says, it's never too late to have a happy childhood.

COMPLIMENTS

Since we have made a list of people who have made negative comments about our bodies, it's only fair to give the other side equal time. There been also people who have said wonderful things about your body. (Don't be surprised if these compliments are harder to remember than the insults you listed in the "Anger" exercise.) Make a list of all the people who have complimented you on the way you look. Write down what they said and how you felt after they said it. Take twenty minutes to compile this list.

AFTER WRITING

Stand in front of a full-length mirror, and read these positive statements out loud to yourself as you look in the mirror. How does it feel to hear phrases like, "You have such pretty eyes," "You've got great legs," "Your breasts are beautiful."?

When someone tells you something positive about your body and you feel good about it afterwards, that is a compliment. Sometimes we get confused if someone tells us something that sounds positive, but we feel uncomfortable about it afterward. For example, when a construction worker whistles and yells, "Nice ass!" that is not a compliment. However, when my lover tells I have a nice ass, I feel good because I know she appreciates me for all sorts of reasons, not just the shape of my anatomy. My lover sees me as a whole person. The same words coming to me from a stranger on the street is an insult, because I feel I am being seen as a "piece of meat," a sexual object, rather than a whole person.

Make sure you feel good about all the compliments on your list as you read them out loud. Are you able to take in that there are people in the world who really do find you attractive? See if you can admit, even to yourself, that you are a beautiful woman. Each of us is beautiful in her own unique way. There are no exceptions (no, not even you!).

HOMEWORK

We don't praise ourselves enough, yet we are so quick to put ourselves down. When someone says to you, "That's a nice jacket," do you say, "Oh, this old thing? I got it on sale for half price, it's really kind of funky," or do you just say, "Thank you"?

Every day this week, after you get dressed in the morning, stand in front of the mirror and compliment yourself. Use your name and be specific. "Lesléa, you look very cute in that red jumpsuit." "Lesléa, that turquoise sweater looks terrific on you. The color is perfect." Feeling good about how you look is important, no matter how much of a feminist you are (at least I think so).

Most people care about their appearance. Most women with eating dis-eases are particularly aware of how they look. See what it's like to take pride in your appearance. No matter what you weigh, you have your own unique beauty.

FAT WOMEN YOU ADMIRE

Think of a fat woman you admire. Describe who she is and what you admire about her. How does she run her life? How does she treat herself and other people? What are the qualities about her you admire the most? What is important to her? How has she affected your life? Take fifteen minutes to write about this wonderful woman. Write without stopping.

AFTER WRITING

Read this "portrait" out loud to yourself. Can you see this woman as a whole person, not just a woman who weighs a certain amount? Can you admire her, respect her and love her, regardless of her body size? Would you love her any more or any less if her body size was different? Probably not. Whenever I get the urge to berate myself by wishing I was thinner, I ask myself, "Would you love so-and-so more if she weighed ten pounds less?" Of course I wouldn't. When I put in the name of someone I love, I see how absurd the question is. So why would I love myself more if I was ten pounds thinner? My weight should be as irrelevant to me as my friend's weight. I love her because she's a wonderful caring person, with a great sense of humor and a heart as big as Mt. St. Helen's. Her weight is completely irrelevant to her worth as a person. So is yours.

HOMEWORK

Describe a different woman you admire and what you like about her every day for a week. At the end of the week, notice the different body types of these seven women. See if the women you picked have a variety of body sizes and shapes, or if they were similar in appearance. What does this information tell you?

IDEAL MEAL

Imagine a perfect meal—a meal that would be nurturing for your body and your soul in all kinds of ways. Where would you eat this meal? Who, if anyone, would you eat this meal with? Set the atmosphere up just right for you. What would you wear? What would your companion(s), if any, wear?

Now for the food. Money is no object, calories are irrelevant. You are limited only by your own imagination. Imagine yourself eating this meal in the most enjoyable way possible. Take the time to give yourself pleasure. When you feel fully satisfied, take twenty minutes to describe this experience and how you feel about it. Write without stopping.

AFTER WRITING

Were you able to really indulge in a satisfying meal or was it hard to give yourself pleasure? Was the scene exotic—a romantic beach, an intimate restaurant—or did you prefer to eat at home? Did your ideal meal include other people, or was it a solitary experience? Did you choose foods that are familiar to you, or new foods? Was there a great variety and quantity of food, or was the meal simple? Did the meal contain foods you usually forbid yourself to have? Did you let yourself have exactly what you wanted?

DISCUSSION AND HOMEWORK

Many of us have deprived ourselves of foods we love for a long time. Or, we have eaten them in secret and felt guilty about it. While food is what we need to ingest in order to survive, it is also a source of pleasure for many reasons—certain foods remind us of pleasant childhood memories, certain foods are very sensual to eat, and certain foods just taste good. Some women, in doing this exercise, find that the food takes a back seat and becomes less important than the other people and the setting of the meal. Other women place all the emphasis on the food. Whatever you did was the right thing for you.

For homework, I'd like you to have the meal you just described, or as close a facsimile as possible. A woman in one of my workshops imagined herself eating pesto on the back of a humpback whale, while a crowd of women out on a whale watching trip all rushed to the side of the boat to admire her. If your ideal meal is as adventuresome as hers, you may have to modify it a bit for reality. Make sure you don't skimp on the pleasure.

NURTURING ACTIVITIES

Make a list of all the things you like to do that have nothing to do with food. Think about your life—what are the little things that give you pleasure as you go through your day? Sometimes the littlest things, such as sitting with a cat on your lap, or having fresh cut flowers in the house, can make us enormously happy. Come up with at least twenty activities that you enjoy doing. This can be an on-going list that you add to over a period of time. Take fifteen minutes to compile your list now.

AFTER WRITING

As women with eating dis-eases, we spend a huge amount of time and energy on food—deciding what to eat and what not to eat, buying and preparing food, scheming about how to eat particular foods when no one is around, fantasizing how wonderful our lives will be when we reach that certain weight. Often, as we get healthier and start obsessing less, we find a lot of extra time on our hands. At this point, a woman with an eating dis-ease has to get to know herself all over again. You may not know what you like to do. That's okay. You can find out.

When I stopped bingeing and purging, I spent a lot of time sitting in my rocking chair and staring at the wall. I was amazed at how much time my destructive eating patterns had taken up. I really didn't know what to do with myself. My biggest fear was that I would sit and stare at that wall forever. But I didn't. Eventually I would get up and call a friend or write a letter or read a book. Eventually I would do something.

I learned that I didn't like things I thought I did. Like going to big parties, for instance. When the lure of the food was gone, I realized that I didn't like being in a crowd of people I didn't know. That doesn't mean I'm a social failure; it means I don't like big parties. That is useful information for me. I found I was participating in activities that I thought I *should* enjoy (*everyone* likes parties). So I stopped. "Should," by the way, is a word that acts like a warning signal to me. If I'm doing something I think I should, chances are I'm doing something I don't really want to be doing at all. Ask yourself, who am I trying to please, by *shoulding* myself?

I started doing things I thought I might like. I had to experiment. I found I like going to the movies by myself. I like reading trashy novels. I don't like gardening. I do like hiking. It took time for me to learn these things.

You are unique. There is no one else quite like you. Take time to find the things you really enjoy doing. Do you like solitary activities like reading and writing? Do you like big social scenes? Do you enjoy being in nature, or in shopping malls? Do you like making things with your hands? Are you intellectually oriented? Do you like foreign movies, great works of art? Are you spiritually oriented? Do you like to meditate? Do you enjoy physical activities, like swimming and biking? Whose company do you enjoy? Do you enjoy doing different things with different friends? Do you have a Scrabble buddy, a movie-going buddy, a special friend you can ask to give you a hug? Be as specific as possible as you add to your ever-growing list.

HOMEWORK

Keep this list handy and add to it every time you
discern an activity that you enjoy. Do at least one
thing on your list every day. If you feel the urge to
binge, do three things from your list and then
decide whether you are going to binge or not. You
may feel differently after taking a bath, playing with
your puppy, or asking a friend for a hug, or you
may feel the same. Whatever choice you make is
fine. If you starve yourself, make sure you do at
least three nurturing things a day when you are
undereating or not eating at all. You may feel more
like feeding yourself afterward, and you may not.
Whatever you decide to do is fine. Practice loving
and accepting yourself, no matter what choices you
make.

A DAY WITHOUT OBSESSING ABOUT FOOD

Imagine you have no issues about food, eating, body image, or weight. You are like a child who is at peace with her body—you eat whenever you are hungry, and you don't think much about food. You like your body just as it is. You are the same age you are right now. If your food obsession was lifted, how would you spend your time? Imagine yourself waking up, getting ready for work or school or play, starting your day. Take yourself through an entire day—a day in your life without worrying about what you will eat or how much you weigh. Start writing now and just let your day unfold, without planning it. Trust your pen. Take at least twenty minutes to do this, and writing without stopping.

AFTER WRITING

Read what you wrote out loud to yourself. Were you able to let your day unfold? Was it different than a day in your actual life? Did you find you had more time? Were you able to do things you wanted to do? How did food fit into the picture? Did you eat meals, snacks, more or less than you usually do? Did you interact with different people than you normally do? How did you feel about yourself? How did you feel when this day was over—relieved, sad, happy, angry? If faced with

another such day, do you think that you would
anticipate it eagerly, or with dread? Write down
your observations.

DISCUSSION AND HOMEWORK

Many women with eating dis-eases find it very
scary to even imagine what it would be like to not
have an eating dis-ease, to be healthy. Having an
eating dis-ease makes your life very predictable. You
start your diet in the morning, blow it in the
afternoon, beat yourself up in the evening, and plan
tomorrow's diet at night. There is no risk-taking
involved. Everything is the same. Painfully so. Yet
we find comfort in the familiar, even the familiar
behaviors that are making us miserable. All change
is scary, even change for the better.

Letting go of an eating dis-ease does not mean
you have to become super-woman. You do not have
to make $100,000 a year, write that novel, have a
perfect relationship, take up a new form of exercise,
and become spiritually enlightened all in the same
week. We women with eating dis-eases have a hard
time being part of the human race, being just
another person on the block. We think we're either
better than everyone else, or more frequently, worse.
It's very scary to stop making those comparisons.
You are not better or worse than anyone else. You
are the same, though of course you are unique. We
are all unique. Women with eating dis-eases are
all-or-nothing types. We either eat everything that
isn't nailed down or we eat nothing at all. Either we
join every extra-curricular activity, volunteer at
thirty organizations, explore fourteen art forms, all
while holding down at least two full-time jobs, or
we do nothing. I invite you to join the human race.

Go to work or to school, have one or two hobbies you enjoy doing, participate in a political or community group. Realize that you have limits. You cannot save everybody and everything. You will also not be happy doing nothing at all. Find your own balance. Moderation is a good principle to practice, with food and in other areas of your life. Not all, not nothing, but something in between.

Pick a day in the coming week to "act as if" you have no issues about food, eating, body image, and weight. See what it feels like to be healthy. See what it feels like to be free. You can experience this, no matter what you weigh. Write about your experience.

TAKING RISKS

Make a list of all the things you've always wanted
to do but are afraid of doing. Take ten minutes to
compile your list.

Read what you wrote out loud to yourself. Pick
one item on your list that you really want to do.
Close your eyes and imagine yourself taking this
risk. Give yourself plenty of time to watch yourself
doing this activity from start to finish. How do you
feel as you are getting ready to try something new?
How do you feel right before you start? What
happens when you are actually involved in the
activity? Do your feelings change as time passes?
How do you feel when you are almost finished?
When you are actually done?

When you are finished, open your eyes and
describe this experience and how you feel about it.
Write for fifteen minutes without stopping.

AFTER WRITING

Read what you wrote out loud to yourself. How
did you feel taking this risk? Were you scared,
excited, nervous, happy, sad, angry? Were you able
to imagine yourself doing this activity from start to
finish? Were you successful in accomplishing what
you wanted to accomplish? If you were, how did it
feel to succeed? If you were not able to complete
this task, can you pinpoint what prevented you
from succeeding? Did your fear stop you? Were you
afraid of succeeding or afraid of failing? Were you

afraid of disappointing someone? Would being
successful be a betrayal of someone? Is "failing" a
way for you to stay connected to someone? If you
were not able to imagine yourself successfully
taking this risk, that does not mean that you
"failed." You learned something new about
yourself, and that is always a success. This
information will be useful to you. Write down your
observations about this exercise.

HOMEWORK

Many women with eating dis-eases are low
risk-takers. Our dis-ease, like any addiction, keeps
us "stuck"—physically, spiritually, and emotionally.
Often our creative energy is stuck. Our careers may
not be advancing the way we would like them to
be. Our financial picture may need improving. We
may be dissatisfied with our relationships.

Eating dis-eases are not just a matter of eating
too little or too much. They are a very effective way
to disrupt your entire life. As you heal, you will
have more energy to put into other areas of your
life. This means doing things you've never done
before.

That is what taking a risk involves. This will
probably be terrifying.

This will probably always be terrifying. But I
have exciting news for you: Courage is doing the
things you are afraid of doing. I always thought
courage meant that you weren't afraid. I've learned
that that's not so.

Having courage means you are afraid of
something, yet you do it anyway. Feeling some fear
and some excitement is a good indicator that the
risk you are about to take is a good one. If you felt

only fear and no excitement, chances are that this
risk is really too scary for you. That's okay. If you
felt only excitement and no fear, that might mean
this risk isn't a big enough challenge for you.

Go down your list and pick two risks that you
are willing to take this week. They don't have to be
tremendous risks like quitting your job and moving
to Alaska, or asking the person you've had a crush
on for three years to go out with you. Wear your
shirt tucked in for half an hour in front of your best
friend. Take yourself out to lunch and eat
something besides a tossed salad with the dressing
on the side. Get a new haircut. Do something that
is not totally terrifying, but something that does feel
a little bit risky. The big risks will still be there a
month from now, or a year from now. You can
work up to them. After you take these risks, either
write about them or talk to a friend or a therapist
about them. Share your successes. They are a gift to
all of us.

MAKING MISTAKES

Imagine yourself in a familiar setting, at work, at school, or in your own home. Picture yourself doing an activity that you often do—hammering a nail, taking a test, feeding your kids lunch. Just some small everyday activity. It doesn't have to be anything extraordinary. As you watch yourself doing this activity, imagine yourself making a mistake—the nail goes in crooked, you answer a test question incorrectly, you put mustard on your daughter's sandwich instead of mayonnaise. How do you feel when you make this mistake? How do you feel afterward? What do you say or do? Take fifteen minutes to describe this experience from beginning to end and how you feel about it. Write without stopping.

AFTER WRITING

Read this piece of writing out loud to yourself. How does it feel to know you're not perfect? Was it a big deal to make a mistake? Did you laugh it off and start over? Did you beat yourself up and let it ruin the whole day? Did you want to binge, starve, or purge because you felt inadequate, stupid, or just not good enough? If you started to get down on yourself, ("I'm so dumb, I'm such an idiot, I can't believe I did that, etc."), try to identify whose voice that is. Does it sound like one of your parents, an old teacher or boss, a sibling, a lover? We are not born hating ourselves. The voice in your head had to come from somewhere. Beating yourself up is a learned behavior. It can be unlearned as well.

How do you treat someone you love when they make a mistake? Do you call them a stupid idiot, or do you just shrug your shoulders and say, "Oh well, everyone makes mistakes"? See if you can give yourself the same space to be human. You are also part of everyone. You don't have to be perfect.

DISCUSSION AND HOMEWORK

Make three deliberate mistakes this week. They don't have to be giant mistakes, like not stopping at a red light and getting into an accident, or figuring wrong and coming up with a $500 error in your checkbook. Try misspelling a word in a letter you write, or wearing mismatched socks. Be ten minutes late to a meeting, or spill some tea on the tablecloth. Notice how you respond to these situations. The more forgiving you are of yourself, the more forgiving you will be of other people as well.

Many women with eating dis-eases are afraid to take risks and try new things because they are afraid of making mistakes. Life is full of mistakes, and at the same time, there are no real mistakes. Everything happens for a reason. If you aren't making mistakes, you probably aren't learning and growing either. Hopefully, as we continue to heal, we make smaller mistakes, and we make new mistakes instead of repeating the same old ones.

I once attended a seminar for women called "Imposters, Fakes, and Frauds" led by Dr. Valerie Young. She informed us that when men start a new job, they think they need to know about 40 percent of what to do in the beginning and that they can learn the other 60 percent. Women, on the other hand, think they have to know 150 percent in order to do a good job! Life is a process of learning, trying, stumbling, trying again, growing, and changing. You don't have to know it all before you begin. If you did, you'd never begin anything!

Write what happens and how you feel about it when you make three deliberate mistakes this week. See if you can be kind to yourself—acknowledge your mistakes, and then let them go.

EXERCISE: THINK ABOUT IT

Picture yourself in your high school gym class. See the outfit or uniform you had to wear; see your classmates and your gym teacher. Pick one sport you remember playing and watch yourself participating in it. Are you inside the gym or out in the field? Is it a team sport or a solo activity? If you are on a team, how do you interact with your teammates? Is anyone watching you? How do you feel about this particular activity while you are doing it? after it's over? Take twenty minutes to describe this experience and how you feel about it. Write without stopping.

AFTER WRITING

Read what you've written out loud to yourself. What kinds of feelings does gym class stir up for you? Did you feel self-conscious in your gym suit? Did you try to get out of class by telling your teacher you had your period? Were you the last picked on the softball team? Or were you the star of the team? Did you hit that last homerun that brought everyone in and won the game? Did you come in last in relay races? Were you always falling off the balance beam? Did your classmates tease you about your athletic abilities, or were they supportive? Were you afraid you were going to get hit in the face with a baseball or fall off the uneven parallel bars, or did each new activity seem like fun? Was your gym teacher supportive? Were you one of her favorites? Or did you cut gym class as often as you dared?

DISCUSSION AND HOMEWORK

Often women with eating dis-eases are not particularly fond of sports. Left to our own devices, we'd be just as happy with a good book (and, as often as not, a big bag of potato chips as well). Most of us did not have cheerleader type bodies in high school, and many of us were teased at any attempts we made at athletic activity. Or, the only physical activity we may have tried was done to augment our dieting attempts—100 sit-ups every night to flatten our bellies, 200 leg lifts to firm our thighs. Ugh. No wonder we hate exercise. Any activity based on self-hate is not going to be fun, I guarantee.

For homework, think of a physical activity that you enjoyed as a kid. It can be very simple; jumping rope by yourself, taking a walk in the woods behind your house, playing TV tag with the other kids on the block, roaming on the beach collecting shells. Children are active beings. There must have been something you liked to do. Write a description of yourself as a child participating in this activity.

EXERCISE: DO IT

Make a list of all the physical activities you've
always wanted to try. They may be as exotic as
skydiving, or as ordinary as jogging. See how many
different kinds of sports you can come up with. The
thought of doing any one of these may be
absolutely terrifying. Write them down anyway.
Take fifteen minutes to compile your list.

Now pick one of these activities and imagine
yourself doing it. Watch yourself get ready—you
might need special clothes like a bathing suit or
tennis shorts. Picture yourself arriving wherever it is
you need to go. Take the time to watch yourself go
through this activity. Notice how you feel from start
to finish. See how you interact with the other
people around you—teammates, spectators,
opponents. How do you feel when the activity is
over?

AFTER WRITING

Read what you wrote out loud to yourself. Can you
imagine yourself actively engaged in a sport? Are
you excited at the thought? Or do you feel scared,
sad, angry? Were you nervous as you got ready to
participate in this activity? Were you anxious, eager,
or terrified? Were you able to imagine yourself
doing well—ice skating gracefully, getting a hole in
one, reaching the top of a mountain? Or did you

strike out, break a leg skiing, or step on your dancing partner's toes? Were the people around you supportive?

Did you have fun, or did this activity seem like a chore? Were you sad or relieved or happy when you were through? Would you want to participate in this activity again?

DISCUSSION AND HOMEWORK

Physical activity is important for everyone not because it will help you lose weight and tighten those flabby thighs—because it gets your heart pumping, your blood going. It helps you feel energized and alive. Many depressed women feel better both physically and emotionally when they start to exercise on a regular basis. Exercise helps many people sleep better too.

Children know the benefits of exercise. They naturally move their bodies throughout the day. We grown-up types often get stuck behind desks or steering wheels and forget we exist from the neck down at all.

For homework, start doing a physical activity that you enjoy. If it's not fun, it doesn't count. If you think 100 sit-ups a night is fun, go ahead, but I'd rather go dancing or canoeing or take a walk in the evening. Try to do some form of exercise three times this week. This doesn't mean you have to exercise three times a week for the rest of your life. Just try it for one week and write down how you feel about it.

With this new information about yourself, begin to incorporate physical activity into your life. Start slowly. When I started training in karate, I went to one class a week. I did this for about six months, and then I started going twice a week. Four years later, I found myself going to three or four classes a week. I know that if I had started with the expectation of going four times a week, I probably would have dropped out within the first month. Be patient with yourself. Especially if you haven't exercised in a long time.

You know what's manageable for you. Start small. Err on the side of caution. You can always build on your successes and do more. See if you can find a friend who might be interested in starting a new hobby with you. You may decide to join an aerobics club or a martial arts center or a volleyball team. Or you may like going for a walk or taking a swim by yourself. Try exercising three times a week, for at least twenty minutes a day for one month and notice if you feel any different. After a month, you may decide you want to continue your "exercise regime" or you may decide it really isn't your bag, and just walking up the street to the mailbox once a day is enough exercise for you. Again, there's no "right" way to exercise, just as there's no "right" way to eat. You decide what's best for you.

KITCHENS

Close your eyes and picture the kitchen of your childhood. See the walls, the table and chairs, the stove, sink, and refrigerator. See the cabinets, cupboards, and drawers. How do you feel, standing in this room? Watch yourself open the cupboards. Notice the pots and pans, the dishes, the food. Open the drawers. Notice the silverware and utensils. Explore every nook and cranny of this kitchen, including the contents of the refrigerator. What feelings come up as you re-discover certain foods, certain cooking tools, certain pictures on the walls? Take twenty minutes to describe what you found and how you feel about it. Write without stopping.

Close your eyes again and picture yourself in the kitchen of the house you live in now. See the walls, table and chairs, the stove, the sink and refrigerator. See the cabinets, cupboards, and drawers. How do you feel standing in this room? Now watch yourself open the cupboards. Notice the pots and pans, the dishes, the food. Explore every nook and cranny of this kitchen, including the contents of the refrigerator. What feelings come up as you come across certain foods or certain cooking tools? Take twenty minutes to describe what you found and how you feel about it. Write without stopping.

AFTER WRITING

Read these two pieces of writing out loud to
yourself. What similarities do you notice? What
differences? Did you feel more comfortable and "at
home" in one kitchen more than the other? How
did it feel to visit the kitchen of your childhood?
Were you happy, sad, angry, or frightened to be
there? What kind of food did you find in the
cupboards and refrigerator? Was there a wide
variety? Was there a lot of junk food or diet food?
Was there hardly any food at all? Did you feel
nostalgic at the sight of your mother's dishes, her
old-fashioned potato masher, or the morning cereals
you used to eat? Was the familiar room a comfort
to you, or did it bring back a flood of unpleasant
memories—tense family meals, secret binges, etc.?
   How do you feel about the kitchen in your own
home? Is it a room that is comfortable for you to
be in? When you imagined yourself in your kitchen,
were you happy, sad, lonely, anxious, scared, or
angry? Are the foods in your kitchen foods that you
enjoy eating, or is your kitchen filled with diet food
or junk food? Or no food at all? Is there a wide
variety of foods to choose from? Are there lots of
utensils and gadgets to cook with? Pretty dishes to
set the table with? Or are your utensils and dishes a
haphazard collection from over the years from
living in different places? Is this a room you feel
good about spending time in, preparing and eating
meals? How does it compare to the kitchen of your
childhood? Write down your observations.

DISCUSSION AND HOMEWORK

The kitchen is the heart of the home. It's the room where we nourish our bodies. But a lot more than that happens in the kitchen. Eating is more complicated than putting gas into a gas tank. Eating has to be psychologically nurturing as well as physically satisfying.

Take twenty minutes to design your ideal kitchen. Take whatever you like from your childhood kitchen and the kitchen in your present home, and incorporate those things into your plan. Do you want a big sunny kitchen with lots of plants in the windows, or a small cooking area and a separate breakfast nook? Do you want lots of modern conveniences, such as a microwave oven and dishwasher, or do you prefer a more old-fashioned kitchen? What kinds of pots and pans do you need? which gadgets? how big a refrigerator? a gas or electric stove? What kind of dishes do you like? place mats or tablecloth? silverware or chopsticks? What will you hang on the walls?

And don't forget the food. What staples do you keep in your house? Grains, pastas, dried nuts and beans, crackers, canned or frozen vegetables, cereals, instant dinners? What fresh foods do you buy weekly—fruits and vegetables, dairy products, meat, chicken, fish, bread? What baking supplies do you need? What dessert items do you want? What do you keep in your freezer, your cupboards, your refrigerator? Remember this is your ideal kitchen. Design it to meet your needs. Maybe you want to keep a box of Poptarts around even though you know they're terrible for you, but they were your favorite breakfast as a kid, and once in a blue moon you get a craving that nothing else will satisfy. Maybe you want an old-fashioned toaster, the kind

that toasts only one side of the bread at a time.
Maybe you want an entire set of stainless steel
knives. Take the time to plan out this kitchen from
top to bottom, making it a room you feel really
good about, a room that will nourish your soul as
well as your body. After you write about it, you
may even want to draw a picture of it.

Part B of this homework is to recreate this ideal
kitchen as much as you can. You probably can't
knock down walls to make the room more sunny or
install a dishwasher and buy a Cuisinart and
microwave all at once. You can, however, get rid of
that rusty old can opener and buy a new one. You
can begin to stock certain foods in your ideal
kitchen. You can buy new place mats. You can
clean out the refrigerator and wash the floor.

Sometimes the littlest things can make the kitchen
seem like a whole new room. I realized that I
automatically took the rubberbands off bunches of
scallions and put them around the doorknob of the
kitchen door, just like all the women of my family
have always done. I always hated seeing those dirty
rubberbands around, and I still do. Why then was I
doing this? Out they went. At the same time, I took
a dish towel my grandmother had given me from
her kitchen and slung it through the refrigerator
door handle. I had seen such dishtowels ever since I
can remember (they have pink flamingoes on them)
and that really made my kitchen feel like home.

I also realized I missed certain foods that I had
grown up with. These "comfort foods" didn't jive
with my "health food" mentality, but they
nourished my soul—gefilte fish, chicken soup with
matzo balls, bagels and cream cheese, chopping
herring—the foods of my Jewish culture. I now eat

them, in moderation, on a regular basis. What are your comfort foods? Do you allow yourself to eat them?

Little by little, turn your actual kitchen into your ideal kitchen, and see what a difference that makes in the way you nourish yourself with food.

CLOTHES SHOPPING

It's that time again. You've looked in your closet, and you have absolutely nothing to wear. Imagine yourself going clothes shopping. Picture yourself getting into your car, or onto the bus or subway, or walking downtown. Do you go alone or with someone? How do you feel on your way to the store? How do you feel as you arrive? Watch yourself pick out some clothing to try on. How do you select your items? How do you feel in the dressing room? Watch yourself remove your own clothes and try on the new clothes. How do you decide what to buy and what not to buy? How do you feel as you look at yourself in the mirror? Watch yourself try on a number of different clothes before you leave. Do you buy anything? How do you feel on the way home?

Take twenty minutes to describe this experience and how you feel about it. Write without stopping.

AFTER WRITING

Read this piece of writing out loud to yourself. Is shopping a pleasant or unpleasant experience for you? On your way to the store, were you anticipating buying something nice for yourself, or were you filled with dread? Did you pick out clothes to try on that you really liked, or were you looking for clothes that would make you look thinner? Did you choose the type of clothing that you always wear, or were you willing to branch out and try new styles? Did you pick bright or dull colors? Solids or prints? Clothes like your mother wears?

How did you feel in the dressing room? Were you able to really look at yourself in the mirror and decide if each article of clothing was right for you? Or were you barely able to face your reflection? Were you upset by the size of the clothing you tried on? Did you choose either sizes that were too large or too small for you, out of habit or wishful thinking? Did you take a long time to try on lots of different clothes, or were you through in five minutes? If you bought something, did it fit you? Or was it something you plan on "growing into?" Or something you want to hide yourself with? Were you happy with your purchase? If you didn't buy anything, how did you feel—sad, angry, relieved, frustrated, tired? How did you feel when you got home? Write down your observations.

DISCUSSION AND HOMEWORK

How we dress is a statement we make about ourselves. Your appearance is important to you, otherwise you probably wouldn't be reading this book. Shopping is often an ordeal, especially for women who are not fashion model thin (in other words, most of us). Over the past thirty years, our culture's standard of "beauty" has changed drastically. Women are now expected to be thinner than ever. Marilyn Monroe, the sex goddess of the fifties, would be considered too fat today! Her gorgeous curves would just have to go. Think about it. The beauty standards of old were large, round, curvy, soft women, like those painted by Renoir and sculpted by Rodin. It's only been in the past few decades that women are supposed to be thin and hard.

Why is this? My theory has to do with feminism, which over the past few decades has been urging women to take up more space and claim our power. It's no coincidence that at the same time we're being told to get "bigger" by feminism the fashion industry and the diet industry is telling us literally to get smaller. Models are thinner (and younger) today than ever before. Women that look like young girls, without full breasts, round bellies, and big hips, are not as threatening as full grown, strong, powerful women.

Clothes are getting smaller as well. Recently I saw a size zero pants at a clothing store. I stared at the size tag for a long time. Who would fit into a size zero? Who would want to? Is the new goal for American women to disappear altogether?

I thought for a while that I was losing my mind, because I experience a size 9/10 of today to be smaller than a size 9/10 of yesterday. Several of my friends have confirmed this observation. Not only that, but I can fit into clothing ranging from a size 7/8 to a size 13/14 without losing or gaining an ounce. Size is irrelevant, just as numbers on the scale are unimportant. What is important is that you feel good about the clothes you are wearing.

Go through your closet and throw out all the clothes that no longer fit you. Get rid of those jeans you wore when you were twelve. Admit that they will never fit you again. Get rid of those chartreuse bell-bottoms you absolutely hate but you've hung onto because they were a birthday present from your Great Aunt Ethel. Make sure every item of clothing you own is a reflection of you, and is something you feel good about putting on your body, whether it's your favorite bathrobe you only wear around the house, or a fancy evening gown.

Part two of this homework is to go shopping (now that you have all that room in your closet) and buy a piece of clothing for yourself. Try and make this a pleasurable experience for you. Think about whether you want to go alone or with someone you trust. Do you want to go to a new store, or one you're familiar with? Maybe you can go shopping and then out to lunch or to a movie. Reward yourself, especially if this is very hard for you.

Some of us have a hard time spending money on ourselves. See if you can let yourself buy something that isn't on sale. I know that many women do not have access to a lot of money and that is something to take into account. At the same time, many of us do not hesitate to spend money on things that will hurt us (binge foods, for example). Yet when it comes to treating ourselves, it is hard to indulge. Be honest with yourself.

Try to treat yourself, even if it's only a new pair of socks. Build a wardrobe that you feel really good about for yourself. Take your time. It will be an on-going process for the rest of your life.

LOVING THE BINGER/
LOVING THE STARVER

Close your eyes and imagine yourself after a binge.
It can be a binge you had yesterday or thirty years
ago. If you do not binge, imagine yourself after a
day of self-starvation. How do you feel physically?
How do you feel emotionally? What do you want?
What do you need?

Now picture yourself as you are today,
comforting the you that just binged or starved. Tell
her it's all right. In fact, thank her for what she just
did. She took care of herself the best way she knew
how, at that moment. She was trying to protect you
from some feelings that she thought were too
painful for you to experience at that moment in
time. She was doing the very best that she could.

Write this part of you a love letter, telling her
how much you appreciate the ways she tried to
protect you and take care of you. Write for twenty
minutes without stopping.

AFTER WRITING

Read this letter out loud to yourself in front of a
mirror, making eye contact with your reflection.
How does it feel to hear these words out loud?
Were you really able to appreciate your "binger" or
your "starver"? Could you feel compassion for her?
Could you love her? Or did you feel angry at her
and want to punish her? Did you judge her? Are
you willing to be friends with her?

144

DISCUSSION AND HOMEWORK

Many of us want to forget the past. Once women with eating dis-eases begin to heal, we want to sigh with relief and say, "Phew, I'm glad that's over." Sorry. This will always be a part of your life. You may never binge, purge, diet, or starve again, but that sad little girl full of self-hate will always be with you. She needs love and care. Many of us want to ignore her. We're angry at her and what she reminds us of. It's very hard for us to love the parts of ourselves we don't even like.

I don't think you will be able to let go of this part of yourself until you fully accept her and even love her. She was very creative and resourceful to think of a way to cope with your particular painful situation, whether that was sexual abuse, having an alcoholic parent, or just the plain loneliness of being a human being on the planet. She thought of bingeing, or bingeing and purging, or starving, all by herself, as a way to keep you safe. And it worked. For a while. Now it doesn't work anymore and you need to find other ways to cope with the pain and the joy of being alive. You can't take away the bingeing/purging/starving behavior without replacing it with something else. I suggest replacing self-hate with self-love. Every day this week do something extra special for yourself. Take a hot bath, call that friend across the country, take yourself out to dinner, buy a new album, get a hug or a massage. See if you can stay in touch with your "binger" or "starver" and give her what she needs. Have her write you a letter and write one back to her. Keep the lines of communication open. It will help you heal and become whole.

AUTOBIOGRAPHY

Imagine yourself at 100 years of age. You have lived a wonderful life, full of all kinds of accomplishments. You've had many satisfying relationships, lots of challenging jobs, and many interesting adventures. You have done most, if not all, of what you set out to do. Now you are nearing the end of your life.

Take twenty minutes to write your autobiography. List the accomplishments you have achieved that make you proud. Looking back over the past 100 years, really think about what you want to be remembered for. Whose lives have you touched? What have you accomplished? Which of your successes were the most important to you? What have you learned? What words of wisdom do you want to leave behind?

AFTER WRITING

Read your autobiography out loud to yourself. Were you able to draw a portrait of the kind of woman you admire? Are you someone you can be proud of? Did you include things you have already accomplished, as well as goals you have not yet met? Was it easy to envision yourself looking back on a full, happy and productive life? Or did you imagine yourself alone, unhappy and a failure? Can you let yourself envision a life you feel good about?

DISCUSSION AND HOMEWORK

When I realized I was going to live in this body for
a long time, my relationship to it began to change. I
no longer have the body of an eighteen-year-old and
I do not yet have the body of an eighty-year-old.
My body is constantly changing, as is yours. I have
slowly let go of controlling these changes. As I get
older I get rounder, wider, more wrinkled. It is
actually a wonderful and wondrous process.

Other things in my life—what I do, who I love,
my work in the world—are more important than
my body size. How many of us really want to be
remembered for our physical appearance? When
you wrote your autobiography, did you write, "Jane
Doe's most significant accomplishment was the fact
that she weighed 105 pounds her entire life?" Or
did you write about the books you wrote, the
children you raised, the work you did with battered
women, the sailboat trip you took around the
world, the black belt you earned in karate? Talk to
old women about their lives. Your perspective on
your body size and how important it is will change
radically.

I taught a creative writing class at a senior center
a few years back, and I was amazed at the beauty
of the old women in my class. Everyone had gray
hair, wrinkles, and glasses. Some of my students
were thin and some were fat. They seemed very at
ease in their bodies. At a certain age (all of these
women were older than 60), you realize you can no
longer look like a sixteen-year-old fashion model,
no matter what you do. There is a tremendous
amount of freedom in accepting your own body.
There are so many other things to focus on besides

what size dress you wear, or how firm or flabby
your belly is. Start pursuing your interests. If you're
like me, you've got a lot of lost time to make up for.

Write a list of your goals for the coming year.
This list should not include wanting to lose a
certain amount of weight or become a certain size.
See if you can put your energy into other things for
now. Then make another list of your goals for the
next five years. For the next ten years. As a friend
of mine says, "If you don't know where you're
going, you're sure to end up somewhere else." This
same friend often tells me, "This is not a dress
rehearsal. This is your life." Start taking small steps
to reach your goals. If you want to be a carpenter,
buy a hammer. If you want to buy a house some
day, open a savings account with a dollar. See if you
can put away a dollar a week toward your goal.
Every little bit counts. You can accomplish your
goals, but it takes time. Just as it is impossible to
lose five pounds in five minutes, it is also impossible
to write an epic poem in one day. Or build a house.
Often our impatience stops us from even letting
ourselves know what we want, let alone try and go
after it.

Your dreams are unique to you. They are a gift to
guide you on your way through life. Nourish them.
Take small steps to accomplish them. You deserve
to have your dreams come true. Your success is a
gift to all of us.

ENDING LETTER

Go back to the letter you wrote to yourself when you first started doing the exercises in this book. It may have been a month ago, a year ago, or longer. Read what you had to say to yourself back then. Now close your eyes and wander down memory lane for a few minutes. Think about the various issues you've explored by using this book. You've talked with various parts of your body, written affirmations, visualized yourself bingeing, talked to the food. You've practiced saying no and asking for what you need. You've re-experienced childhood meals, meals eaten alone, meals eaten with friends and lovers. You've explored issues around anger, sexuality, body size, exercising, and clothing. You've established a relationship with the sad little girl full of self-hate who lives inside you. You've worked very hard. How is the you of today different than the woman who first bought this book?

Write yourself a letter in which you talk about the experiences you've had with this book. Write for twenty minutes without stopping.

AFTER WRITING

Read what you've written out loud to yourself, in front of a mirror, making eye contact with your reflection. Are you proud of yourself for all you've done? Were you able to give yourself credit where credit is due? Or are you dissatisfied because you aren't perfect yet? Do you measure your success in pounds lost or gained, or in emotional and spiritual recovery? Is your body size and weight less important to you now than it was when you first cracked open this book? or is it more important? Have your eating habits changed? Is your wardrobe different? Do you spend less time thinking about food and body size? Have you made changes in any of your relationships? Taken a new job? Started a new hobby? Begun to play a new sport?

Focus on your successes. Even one small step, like not calling yourself an idiot after eating something you wish you hadn't, is worth applause. You are working hard to change lifelong patterns, and that takes a tremendous amount of courage. Just buying this book or taking it out of the library or borrowing it from a friend is an act of self-love. Mazel tov. Your healing has begun. The seeds have been planted. Your homework is to be good to yourself, to nurture and cherish yourself, just as you are, for the rest of your life. Start by looking in the mirror and smiling. This is the hardest assignment anyone will ever give you. Also the most rewarding. You can do it.

ANTHOLOGY

The following pieces were written by women who have participated in my workshops What Are You Eating/What's Eating You? The authors are fat and thin, old and young, lesbian and heterosexual, Jewish and gentile, women of color and white women, all in different stages of their recovery. All of these women (including myself) have one thing in common: a desire to stop hating our bodies. I find this writing very moving and inspiring. I hope you do too.

I used to think that if I closed my mouth on words and let the silence grow unchecked for too long, my lips would seal like a healing sore. I pictured a thin lined scar in a desert sun. I talked a lot to the silence that grew in my room as I grew. We fought for control in the closet space at night. I used the stars and the moon to help me win. At dinner my mother would tell me to clear my plate. I never answered her and always left the table with my napkin full. I held my stomach in the palm of my hand.

Beth Peckman

Bodies at the Y

bodies
naked bodies
fleshy white naked bodies
pillow soft naked bodies
blue veined naked bodies
ripe swelling naked bodies
curly haired naked bodies
sleek spare naked bodies
curving bodies
loose bodies
swaying bodies
browned bodies
full bodies
firm bodies
stringy bodies
budding bodies
shy naked bodies
open naked bodies
lovely naked bodies all
woman bodies all
even mine
bodies
all

Beautiful

Linda Shaughnessy

The Sculpture of My Body

Light brown sandstone landscape . . . sculpted by the
Goddess . . . rolling thundercloud shoulders pour
powerful into the curve of strong arms. Dark hair
raining, showering over the clouds wild and free . . .
mounds of mother breast joined smooth to chest . . .
armpit forest pit tangle of shrub, earth scent lingers .
. . belly soft, folds meet hanging breast, folds
insulation, snow over the forest floor, added warmth
gently rolling past belly into tangle thicket, forest
primeval . . . wet hidden fruits peek out, apples and
pears exposed to the sun . . . leaning out hips jiggle
when touched . . . soft springy moss ground . . .
down down the pillars of gentle stone . . . legs large
muscles loom, ancient mountain range hidden in
clouds . . . climb down to the calves, so many curves,
a rolling farmland . . . hair like corn stalks cover the
land . . . feet emerge heels sturdy . . . mounds of
flesh, supple strong ass, Indian mounds, sacred
treasure climbing over mounds to the prairie of my
back, swim through the hair and find your way back
. . . see the light brown sandstone again.

Angel Russek

Monologue from My Thighs

Thunder thighs you called me, for years, yeah and I
remember you sitting on the toilet and with your
finger as an imaginary knife, cutting away from me
all you didn't want, joking to this day that in the
next life you want long legs, good teeth and a big
bladder, you are always scrutinizing my shape and
size and sure that I am the largest in the room no
matter how many other sizes and shaped bodies may
be present. You never ever let me wear shorts, even
running in summer. You're either pinching me or
ignoring me or hopelessly glancing at me.

Well, you know what? I am incredibly strong. I
give you a lot of support, literally, just walking on
this earth, the strength and stability of these legs have
led you on many wonderful journeys giving you
endless pleasurable runs through cornfields, given
your hips, pelvis, torso the ground to dance many a
drum. I don't get sick. I don't complain. I am the
result of your abuse, not the cause of it. Why is
round bad? Why is large bad? Who said we had to
be long, lanky legs or little petite ones? We are
peasant stock here, on the earth, made for walkin'
and dancin' and lovin', not for perfect image making,
whatever that is. There is power in us and you know
it. You can't just have our power without accepting
our shape as well.

Carolyn Sadeh

Love Poem to My Feet

Oh sweet feet!
You always stand by me
in the yard, on the street.
You archless wonders,
flat as pancakes—
the shoe salesman clicked his tongue in dismay,
I told you not to let your feet spread,
he said, reaching up for orthopedic saddle shoes
which you burst apart at the seams!
Oh mighty feet
spread yourself far and wide
like vicious rumors, like juicy gossip,
like Skippy's peanut butter!
Oh you two fleshy foots
you knew long before I did
how important it is to take up space
make your place in this world,
none of this pussyfooting around
none of this tiptoeing through the tulips for you!
You wouldn't squeeze into a pair of 6 inch
heels for nobody,
knowing there was no Prince Charming
waiting around for you.
You wanted to smash his glass slipper
the way my brother smashed a wine glass
under his foot at his wedding
while you wiggled your toes in secret delight
hidden by the tablecloth
free of those sky blue pumps dyed to match my
    gown.
Oh feet
with your ten toes and ten toenails
with your calluses, mosquito bites
and occasional athlete's foot,

I will knit you woolen mukluks
to keep you warm all winter,
I will let you run barefoot and wild all summer
and weave daisy chains between your toes,
I will anoint you with sandalwood oil
and pay a fortune for a pedicure, a massage,
a pair of homemade leather sandals,
a portrait of you to hang on my wall
Oh feet
spread your ten toes wide
don't let them fence you in
your stride is wide
your steps are firm
you have important work to do
carry me around this earth.

Lesléa Newman

Love Poem to My Belly

You are soft and curved as the wind in summer
strong and hard as the wind in winter
You carry love as lightly as the snow
All the loves of my life
and all the babies
who are now grown and gone
You move in the rhythm of the dance
moving with my breathing
in and out
deep and soft
forever

Jay Goldspinner

O little Buddha belly
so soft and loveable
many nights I have spent
with my hands resting
on your warm roundness

As soft warm breath
enters my body
you rise and fall
with the ease of
the ebb and flow
of the ocean tides

So magnificent is
your unique beauty
as you travel the world
and change color
in the golden sunshine

Your naked splendor
is something to behold
as you lie in a bubble bath
feeling the bubbles
lie gently upon your loveliness

O little Buddha belly
so soft and loveable
many more nights will I spend
with my hands resting
on your warm roundness

Hania Cennerazzo

To My Gut

Strange, exotic, scary, lonely thing—
I wouldn't let anyone see you, touch you,
come close.
Sometimes I would look at you
with revulsion, fascination, awe . . .
That you are so brave as to exist at all
Sometimes makes me wonder.

That you love me, care for me, protect me,
endure me,
I am secure in these things.
Do you feel loved by me?
You trust me no matter what I do.
You're always there.
You don't go away.
You persevere, faith unwavering.

Thank you.
I do love you.
I am sorry.

I am forgiven.
And that is hard.

Carolyn Arnold

Directions

When you hear yourself say
ten pounds. Summer's coming
or spring. Or vacation
I'm gonna lose it
this time
for good
when you feel your fingers
grab at your stomach
like a sharp-beaked pigeon
at a hunk of leftover hamburger roll
or your fists pound your thighs
(these are not ugly words,
"stomach" "thighs"
hummingbirds, mermaids, babies in utero,
unicorns, E.T.,
people in love,
even happy folks have them
stomachs and thighs . . .)
When you hang up your heart on those
"Losing Those Ten Pounds" blues
this is what you must do. Choose one.

Leave
two sacks of sugar
out in the rain.
Put forty-three tenpenny nails
in a can. Drop it off of a step ladder
into tall grass.
Pour 1.5 gallons of orange juice
into a jug with a slow leak.
Toss a ten-pound note on the dashboard, then
drive down the highway at seventy-five
with the windows open.
Feed one-hundred-sixty-two quarters

into a coke machine
out of order.
Jump into a lake
then take off your wet clothes.
Hang two shirts, a striped sock,
and three pairs of jeans
out to dry in a hurricane.
Leave your gold rings and necklaces
diamonds and deeds
and the difference in pennies
piled on the beach
within reach of the tide.

Know it by now
Any ten pounds
of you
is too precious
to lose.

Linda Shaughnessy

Monologue from the Food's Point of View

I am a chocolate candy bar. Milk chocolate with squares filled with raspberry cream. I was made in Germany by loving hands, then wrapped in paper and sent to the U.S. For a long time I traveled in dark, cold boxes; I felt unwanted and unloved. At last I was placed on a grocery store shelf. I enjoyed the light, the bustle of people walking by. So imagine my excitement when one day Anne picked me up and placed me in her grocery cart. Ah, I thought, I'm going to a new and loving home. Into the bag I went, then into the great outdoors, snuggled with the other groceries. She put the bag in the car and then began to poke inside it and feel around until she found me. She pulled me out and put me on the car seat. I was so pleased to be singled out. She started the car, began to drive away, and then picked me up and began to unwrap the paper. There I was, naked and exposed. Well, imagine my surprise when I suddenly found myself being thrust into her mouth! Ouch, pieces of me were being bitten off! I was sucked and licked and swallowed down the deep dark tunnel of her throat. Yuk, into that disgusting pit of a stomach, there to mix with all kinds of stewing garbage. Oh Mother, if you could only see me now! Where are you when I need you? More disgusting food keeps tumbling in on top of me. Ah, at last I'm being pushed out into another tunnel. It's not all that quiet here, but compared to the factory I just escaped from, this is a relief. Pushing along here, trying to move the crap in front of me, being pushed by the crap behind me. What a disappointing life this has been. Kerplop!

I just landed in an outhouse hole! I think I'll be quite happy just to lay here and compost. Next time around I don't plan to be a chocolate bar!

Anne Perkins

My Hunger

I am an octopus who lives in her heart. I have
hundred of limbs reaching from her rib cage through
her arms, hips, back, neck, legs and brain. My limbs
are electrified nerves which dance frantically in all
directions, squirming through her body—needing,
needing, needing. I don't mean to make her
uncomfortable and annoyed, but I need my thirst
quenched. I have boundless energy; she sedates me.
She tells me to be quiet, "shhh," she says. She
sandpapers my limbs away with food. It stifles my
activeness, it injures my arms and legs. It temporarily
stunts my growth. But then I'll start again. My limbs
start wiggling spastically and uncontrollably
throughout her body.

   I live in her heart. I am her heart. I am a large grey
organ that pumps powerfully. I make a thundering
sound and I am heard. I turn deep purple sometimes
and I pump slower. At times I pump so slow, I cry. I
whimper. My purple skin turns blue.

   I try desperately to yell. Words never come out. My
mouth opens like a baby bird waiting for worms
from mom. I reach and reach unsuccessfully trying to
scream. It's like one of those dreams when you try
and shriek but you cannot. There's just a huge yelp
for help with echoes through hollow walls.

                                                Anonymous

Letter From My Hunger

I am tight, so tight and aching, and wanting in you,
your chest and throat and jaws, spreading like a
pyramid to your mouth. The ache is a constriction,
an exhale, not let go, a fiery purple of passion, of
wanting the whole wide world and right now and in
every direction. Running here and there, being there
for people, talking out anything to not let it build up,
the tightness of want, reaching empty arms out,
holding the tightness over the pressure from below of
wanting to throw up and feel the moment's peace
that follows, to get to the release I can have in my
chest after crying, crying. Such a clear feeling like
after running, not like after eating. The hunger is not
in my belly but I fill it so as to distract from the
aching in my chest. If you keep the belly full the rest
of the body stays numb, coping and not allowing the
waves and waves of sadness out, the overwhelming
layers into what aloneness is.

Mary Chester

A Description of My Mother Eating

We're sitting at the dining room table—polished mahogany that Aunt Hazel gave her years ago—and she's always worried about getting a scratch on it. There are tan straw place mats, greenish bowls full of salad (lettuce and sprouts). The pink flowered dishes have a broiled hamburger patty, a piece of toast and a garnish. The silverware shines; the glasses too.

Mom sits eating and talking animatedly about politics. She wears a flowered blouse, the buttons pull over her large breasts. Her white hair is curled and combed. Her thin wrists with the thin blue watch band, her thin fingers with her diamond ring, handle the fork easily, casually, gracefully. Her body sits tightly in her chair—she is as at ease as she knows how to be—never a slouch or a humped shoulder—but not really rigid. M. described her as from a world of gentile poverty and there is truth to it, for though she's never had money, she loves expensive things, in moderation of course.

The food she eats is 100% healthy. She does not like fat, taught me not to like it. She never interferes, never tells me to lose weight, but when I'm thin she tells me over and over how good I look and when I'm fat she tells me over and over how proud she is of me.

Anonymous

My Mother Eating a Meal

Prepare, prepare, prepare and make a point of telling
everyone how much you prepared, how wonderful it
tastes, how little time it took you . . . and you still
prepare. Stay in the kitchen, one course behind the
rest of us. You were eating shrimp cocktail, everyone
else their soup. Your soup was cold and we were all
eating spaghetti. You used food as your way of
showing your love, and how you LOVED to show
love, my dear mother. The pies and cheesecakes, the
homemade spaghetti and gravy simmering all day.
Your love. And you never got to fully love yourself,
always one step behind everyone else. Rushing to get
the dishes from one course done before sitting down
to the next. Where was the time for you to sit, relax,
and enjoy your own wonderful magical cooking? You
refrained from telling me you loved me but you
knew (and know) no end to nurturance with food. I
love food because of you. Maybe here is the heart
and belly converging, dear mother. Your heart was
hiding among the green beans, peeking out at me
from under slabs of white meat turkey. Your heart,
hidden in the stuffing and I swallowed it, chewed it,
and learned to take your glorious food into my heart
space, not my belly. Did you enjoy those meals?
Hunched over, eating fast, always busy doing
something else in the kitchen? What did Grandma
teach you? She never cooked meals for us, only you.
Where did you learn to express love? You found food
as your outlet and I ate it. But now I need to separate
my heart from my belly . . .

Angel Russek

My Mother Eating a Meal

There she sits at the kitchen table in an old smock
dress bent over her plate. The whole family is there,
yet she sees no one. Her focus is on the plate of
raviolis in front of her and she's shoving them in as
fast as she can, wondering if others are watching her.
She loves this food of her heritage, her childhood, yet
she is angry at it for getting her fat. She eats melba
toast and cottage cheese in the morning, hating every
bite yet believing it's what she needs to do. So now
she takes more ravioli and returns to her special seat
at the table. She's a little bit hunched over her plate
and eats without looking up. When she's finished
with the raviolis she goes to the candy cabinet to get
a sweet. She chooses a Milky Way and stands leaning
against the counter, eating it. She looks unhappy, like
she's denying something. I wonder how her sex life is.
Was she unhappy in this marriage and eating for
solace? Her body is similar to mine: skinny legs,
round belly, abundant breasts and a round face. She
never did seem to like her body. Always shopping at
Lane Bryant and wearing clothes that were tent-like
so you couldn't tell what was under there, and yet she
always told me in a negative way that if I was fat no
one would like me. Did she feel unloved? How did
she see herself? She thought so little of herself that
she created a dis-ease that killed her at forty-four. I
don't want to carry my mother's weight. I can love
and support my father, sisters and brother without
carrying her weight. She asked me to take care of the
family when she died and this is the weight I am
carrying, that's it. I'm carrying this weight for her.
What pain I feel in my solar plexus at this moment.
This weight can be carried in another way. Everyone
is grown now and so am I, except for that

fifteen-year-old who wants her mother, who misses her mother terribly, who feels she missed something by not having a mother to grow into adulthood with. Ma can I give up this weight I accepted from you?

Hania Cennerazzo

Ways to Nurture Ourselves Without Food

▲ Go for a walk
▲ Listen to music
▲ Sing
▲ Write a letter
▲ Read a good book
▲ Visit or call a close friend
▲ Paint or draw
▲ Play with clay
▲ Look at a map of the world (or a globe) and imagine yourself in an exotic place
▲ Fantasize
▲ Light candles in the dark, and play Mozart
▲ Give and receive a massage
▲ Take off all your clothes and put your favorite lotion on
▲ Take a bath with or without a book
▲ Massage your feet
▲ Call a special friend to talk, ask them over for tea or to do something special
▲ Call a special friend who's far away to say hi
▲ Doodle, write, paint, just create in general
▲ Meditate
▲ Put music on and dance around your room
▲ Dress up for yourself and stay home or go out to the movies
▲ Light lots of candles around your room and drink tea
▲ Burn incense
▲ Start a book you want to read for pleasure, or read a chapter in one you've started
▲ Take a walk with someone's borrowed pet dog, or alone

▲ Organize your room, your belongings, your clothes, clean out old junk, decorate, refurbish it with new
▲ Take a long drive in your car with your favorite tapes
▲ Dress up in front of the mirror, try new make up and hairstyles
▲ Go out in the porch and write in the dark
▲ Curl up in bed with a good book
▲ Give yourself a facial
▲ Sit in a jacuzzi
▲ Take photos
▲ Go for a bike ride
▲ Go swimming
▲ Go to sleep
▲ Take a walk in the woods, or somewhere peaceful
▲ Make a list of affirmations or read one made before
▲ Do yoga
▲ Kiss and hug your cats
▲ Kiss and hug your lover
▲ Chant
▲ Take a hot shower
▲ Browse in a bookstore
▲ Talk to a close friend about how you feel
▲ Listen to your favorite music
▲ Go shopping
▲ Go "people watching"
▲ Go to a museum
▲ Love something—an animal or person
▲ Read your favorite children's book
▲ Hug someone you wouldn't ordinarily hug
▲ Wash your hair or someone else's or have someone brush yours
▲ Practice karate
▲ Lie on the couch naked
▲ Sew

▲ Punch your pillow
▲ Cry
▲ Suck your thumb
▲ Masturbate
▲ Ask to be held
▲ Color in a coloring book
▲ Go to the hot tubs
▲ Make a list of everything you are grateful for
▲ Lie around and do nothing and don't feel guilty
▲ Buy yourself flowers
▲ Remember everything you like about yourself
▲ Give your cat a neck massage
▲ Practice juggling
▲ Buy yourself herbal cosmetics that will make you
    feel healthy, beautiful and well taken care of
    whenever you use them, and use them
▲ Go out and buy yourself a very sexy article of
    clothing that fits you right now

One Spring[*]

The air was thick with the promise
of lilacs and rain that evening
and the clouds hovered about my shoulders like
the mink stole in my mother's closet I tried on
from time to time.
I was sixteen and I knew it.
I tossed my head like a proud pony
my hair rippling down my back in one black wave
as I walked down the sultry street
my bare feet barely touching the ground
past the sounds of a television,
a dog barking,
a mother calling her child,
my body slicing through the heavy air like a
    sailboat gliding on lazy water.

When the blue car slowed alongside me
I took no notice
until two faces leaned out the open window.
"Nice tits you got there, honey."
"Hey sweetheart, shine those headlights over
    here."
"Wanna go for a ride?"
I stopped,
dazed as a fish thrust out of water
into sunlight so bright it burns my eyes.
I turn and walk away fast
head down, arms folded,
feet slapping the ground.

* This poem is a response to people who made derogatory
  comments about my body one spring.

I hear, "Nice ass, too,"
then laughter
the screech of tires
silence.

All at once I am ashamed of my new breasts
round as May apples
I want to slice them off with a knife
sharp as a guillotine.
All at once I am mortified by my widening hips
I want to pare them down with a vegetable
peeler until they are slim and boyish.
All at once I want to yank out my hair by the
    roots
like persistent weeds that must not grow wild.
But I am a sensible girl.
I do none of these things.
Instead I go home, watch TV with my parents
brush my teeth and braid my hair for the night.
And the next day I skip breakfast,
eat an apple for lunch
and buy a calorie counter,
vowing to get thinner and thinner
until I am so slim I can slip
through the cracks in the sidewalk
and disappear. And I do.

Lesléa Newman

A Family Dinner From My Adolescence

It's five o'clock. The kitchen is a clamor of pots and pans being jostled about, crackling noises from the flank steak broiling in the oven, and the klunk of Mom's cleaver against the cutting board. On the stove, broccoli sits in a pot of water waiting to be boiled; the only thing at rest in the entire kitchen. Rice simmers on a neighboring burner. Upstairs, I am laboring over a new poem and avoiding my history paper, my thoughts competing with Ethel Merman blasting from my brother's stereo in the next room. Amidst the kitchen smells, Mom's voice comes sailing up the stairs like an arrow, piercing my thoughts.

"Rose?" From the urgency of her voice, one would think the house had caught fire.

"Yes?" I yell back, swallowing back my frustration, because I'm well acquainted with the fury I would meet with, were I to page her from another room.

"How would you like to make a salad?"

I know it's not a real question. It never is. *Not particularly* I'd like to yell down, but I know better. This isn't a request, it's a test of my love. I grit my teeth and respond with a distracted, "Sure, just let me finish my thought."

Ten minutes later my mother bellows from the bottom of the stairs, "I guess I'll have to do it myself."

Though there's a good two hours before dinner, I know that if I don't report to the kitchen immediately the salad will be made when I arrive and Mom will use it as evidence in a future argument that I have no respect for her time or her work and everyone "shits all over her" and expects her to be the maid. So I close my pen into my journal, trot to the kitchen and explore the cabinets and refrigerator for interesting salad ingredients. I settle on a Caesar because a) it always goes over well, and b) this is one of the nights Dad is coming home and Mom likes to have his favorite foods on the menu.

While I'm taking my time over the salad, Mom grades papers in the living room. She seems not to be anxious for Dad's arrival, but her rhythmic chewing on her reading glasses gives her away. Soon she will fix herself some cheese and crackers and a drink; a ritual they used to share.

At seven o'clock the rumble of the garage door announces Dad's arrival. The car door opens and slams. Dad walks in through the back door and gives me a kiss. His cheeks are cold. "Oooh, Caesar salad. How's the history paper?" he asks on his way to greet Mom and hang up his coat.

"I don't know," I mumble into the salad.

"Rose, call Louis in for dinner."

After my third attempt to shout to Louis over Broadway's newest releases, the music stops and Louis emerges.

"You don't have to scream at me," he grunts as he drags himself down the stairs to the dinner table.

None of us wants to be there. I wonder why we even bother anymore. Masochist that she is, Mom feels this need to cater to Dad's unyielding sense of family, and Louis and I are part of the act.

Everyone is gathered around the table except me. Mom and Dad sit at the two heads, Louis sits at one of the long sides, opposite my empty place.

"Start without me," I yell from the kitchen. I am busily fixing the most effortless vegetarian alternative I know: Scrambled Eggs A La Rose. I scoop the eggs, some rice, and a little broccoli onto my plate, hold my breath and carry my dinner to the table.

"Looks delicious," Mom comments sarcastically. "Too bad *I* have to eat steak."

"Yes, it is too bad," I respond, picking up my fork and staring down at my plate.

Dad shovels his food in large mouthfuls, I eat in smaller faster ones, Mom picks nervously and Louis just moves the food around on his plate.

Dad begins to discuss office matters, when Mom puts her fork down with a sudden gesture and look of alarm on her face.

"The rolls! They're burning in the oven!"

"God damn it," Dad hollers. "How can anyone be so oblivious?"

Mom rushes to the kitchen to rescue the rolls. It is too late. The pan sizzles as she runs water over the hardened black loaves. She scrapes the rolls into the garbage, turns on the fan and comes back to her seat at the table. She doesn't pick up her fork, but just sits rigid and stares out of startled eyes like a trapped animal. Dad and I continue eating, and Louis continues to stir his food around on his plate. He belts out a few spontaneous bars of *Anything Goes,* screeching to a halt when Dad glares in his direction. Mom begins eating slowly, which she only does when she's lost her appetite. Meanwhile, my appetite is growing voraciously.

"Too bad you can't write history papers as fast as you can eat," Dad says with his mouth full of food.

I put down my fork. I watch Mom take one last bite of food before she cups her hand over her mouth and gags. She springs from the table and runs up the stairs to her bathroom.

"God damn it!" Dad shouts at no one.

Everyone is silent. Dad finishes his meal.

"I'm sorry kids," he says, as he pulls his chair back, gets up and slowly walks up the stairs.

"It's your turn to do the dishes," Louis mumbles.

I say nothing. Louis gets up, saunters into the living room and turns on the TV.

After stuffing the rest of my dinner into my mouth, I clear the table. Alternately I scrape the plates into the trash and into my mouth. As I'm washing dishes I shove a few of the cookies that were supposed to be dessert into my mouth. Soon everything is clean except the rice pot. Before I squirt blue soap into the pot, I scrape the sides and eat the remaining rice off the serving spoon.

When all the counters are sponged down and everything is put away, I pour myself a tall glass of milk, 3/4 full. I take the bottle of Kahlua from the liquor cabinet and fill my glass the rest of the way up. In the clear plastic glass with the daisy on the front, it looks just like chocolate milk. I trudge up the stairs with my camouflaged drink and plant myself at my desk. I glare at my history book. With one violent sweeping motion, I shove it to the floor. I take a long, soothing swallow of the velvety liquid and open my journal. I will make several trips into the kitchen for refills, before I shut my eyes at 3:00 a.m.

Rose Inbloom

A Meal With A Lover

We are walking in town. It's late evening and we are waiting for a 9:00 movie.

"I'm starving," he says. "Are you hungry? I haven't eaten all day. Let's go get something to eat. C'mon."

What? He hasn't eaten all day? Why not? He's so skinny, he can't afford not to eat. I, on other hand, could do with several days, weeks without eating. But do I? No, only sometimes, but certainly not today. Today I have eaten all day. I don't want to eat anymore. I'm not hungry. I shouldn't be. I had planned to skip dinner tonight; I assumed he would have eaten already. What do I tell him? He needs to eat, but he'll expect me to eat as well. Can't he see I certainly don't need to eat? If I tell him I'm skipping dinner tonight he'll get angry. "What? Lisa, you have to take better care of yourself—you have to eat something." Or if I tell him I'm not hungry, then he'll insist, "Come on. Here—have just a little. It's good." But I could never admit to him that I'd already stuffed myself to the gills today and if I eat anymore, why I very well may throw it all up. No, no I can't tell him that. He never eats sugar in front of me. Sometimes he forgets and exclaims his desire for ice cream or chocolate brownies, but then quickly apologizes and says it's a good thing he's with me cause that stuff's not healthy anyway. Oh well, I'm glad I can keep him away from his wicked temptations. If I could only do so well myself.

"Come on. I'll buy you a slice."

Oh, what am I going to do? I don't want to just sit and watch while he chows down a greasy, slimy, cheesy piece of pizza. I don't want him to think I've eaten so much that I am avoiding food. I don't want him to think I am concerned about my weight when he so obviously isn't. I don't want him to think that food is an issue for me when he can be as blasé as he is. I am quiet. All this time we've been walking and now standing in front of the pizza place, I have not said anything. He interrupts my thoughts once more.

"Well, come on. Are you hungry or not?"

That's not such a simple question. Hunger really has nothing to do with it.

He opens the door and walks in. For a second I linger behind, then follow.

"Two slices, please," he orders at the counter. Then he turns to me. "What do you want to drink?"

Lisa Jahn-Clough

Anger

Sad, afraid, depressed, but not that, not ANGRY! For what reason do I have to be angry, surely having endured twenty years of being called fatso, whale and tank is not reason enough. Going out with friends and not being able to fit in the chair is not reason enough. What about spending time educating a friend about fat oppression, only to have her comment in front of you about fat and lazy people, as if the two are interchangeable? What about a male sibling asking you if you're a lesbian because you're fat, perhaps it's easier to find a woman to love than a man? Are we as women second best—I THINK NOT!!!

What if you are told that it is better to accept the horror of surgery to staple your stomach with its three-percent mortality rate ("it really is not much of a risk") than to live as a fat woman; does that entitle me to be angry? Is being abused and raped as a child reason enough? How about living in a culture that devalues women? Is it reason enough to have faced trying to extinguish your life and having failed? WHAT, TELL ME, IS REASON ENOUGH TO GET ANGRY?

S.A.D. Endangered Spirit

Shopping

Fashionless pieces of cloth seemingly hide the bulk of my body. I am twelve and already in adult clothes, clothes made with grandma in mind. I have entered the world of "Specialty Stores." Stores for children/women who are considered to be of proportions beyond what is normal. Meaning we pay and pay more money for less clothes. Meaning being bombarded by voyeuristic sales people, "Excuse me dear, *What* size did you say you wear!!!" and "Such a young face," with my mind finishing their thought, "for such a huge body."

For days I would have to gear myself up for this type of oppression, wondering why thin people who hated fat people would work at these stores. The inevitable "May I help you?" was met with panic, trembling and cold sweats. At that time I didn't know the word NO was a right of mine. I felt that I had no rights! As I tried to make my body less than it was so that these rags would fit, I knew that the ever cheerful salesperson would be waiting outside for me. Soon I would hear "Come on out here and take a look at yourself." Of course it was a three-sided mirror. *MOM help me!!!!!!* Mirrors, doors, windows, people have taught me to hate what I see in them—myself.

I have aged with this oppression and the hatred has increased as my size has. There are no longer stores for me to shop in. I AM NONEXISTENT. My spirit has left my body, her attempt at survival. No longer spirit in human form, only human form. Form that is battered by this world every waking moment, that cries for its right to exist, be seen and be heard.

S.A.D. Endangered Spirit

Declaration

Not my mother's
to dress and curl
and withhold cupcakes from
and be aghast and sorry
about its size.
My Body.

Not my lover's
to carry off to darkness
and break into a frenzy
and be aghast and sorry
about it being the first time.
My Body.

Not my husband's
to undress and occupy
like territory deeded
and be aghast and sorry
that I didn't like it.
My Body.

I'm not aghast,
I'm not sorry,
having gotten to this place
throwing fans of fingers
big as I am
into the sky crying

yes, my daughter, suckle.
I am pleased to share
when I am pleased to share
my body.

Jessamyn Lee

Ideal Meal

It is five o'clock on the day both our lovers have left
on a three-month-long field study. Jasmine and I sit
beside a crackling fire in a small New England
cottage. We sit cross-legged on square floor pillows
stuffed with cotton batting. A hand-carved rosewood
table squats between us, low to the floor. On it, a
purple candle sheds yellow light on a watercress and
endive salad garnished with warm slices of fresh goat
cheese and seasoned with a light mustard dressing.

Closing our eyes, we clasp hands and focus on our
breathing, then on the sweet sound of the flute music
emanating from the little phonograph in the other
room, and finally on our excitement about sharing
this meal together. We can smell the squash cooking
in the kitchen, as we munch first on a crispy bite of
watercress then on the softness of the cheese, little
moans of pleasure escaping between mouthfuls.

When we complete our salads, we talk a little
about Ron and Dave and social ecology, as we await
our second course.

Fifteen minutes later, Jasmine goes to the kitchen
and takes the millet-butternut croquettes from the
oven. She scoops two onto each plate, ladles carrot
sesame dressing over the top and sets them on the
table. In separate bowls, she serves brown rice and
chestnuts and squash and turnips laced with ginger
burdock sauce.

I am quiet for a moment before I pick up my
chopsticks. The croquettes are baked round and soft
and yellow, like smooth breasts. I take a bite, and it
glides like velvet on my tongue. "Mmm," I sigh,
knowing this food could feel nothing but good inside
my stomach.

Though I pause to gaze appreciatively at my friend, I hardly speak until I have finished. The nutty flavor of the rice is grounding and the sweetness of the vegetables, over which I have sprinkled toasted sesame seeds, complement the meal well. I leave some squash in my dish and a little rice in my bowl to save room for dessert.

While Jasmine clears the table, I put a new record on the phonograph. Then we laugh, gossip and philosophize, as the music sings gently to our digestive systems. Soon our voices are lulled by the flute into comfortable silence.

We look at one another and giggle because we know it is time to unveil the dessert. I go to the kitchen and retrieve my surprise "Ta-dah!" Jasmine gasps as I set before her a dense slice of carob fudge pie topped with a fluffy layer of carob tofu custard. We giggle and eat, pause, then eat and giggle.

Rose Inbloom

The Perfect Meal

I am with my new lover. We are on the patio of a
large, secluded, English country mansion bequeathed
solely to us for the evening from a well-endowed
elder friend who views the procurement of passion as
a fine art.

In this huge mansion, only a slim male waiter can
be seen. He is a young, innocent, muscular man,
dedicated to serving women of particular persuasion.
He wears a simple black tuxedo.

The patio, shaped like a half-moon, overlooks a
wide meadow encircled by tall pines and graced with
an oval, mirror-like pond, where two white swans
peacefully glide. A nearby willow dances her leaves in
the cool evening breeze. It is mid-summer at dusk; the
sun slowly setting over the horizon, replacing itself
with brilliant hues of orange, pink and lavender. A
light mist gently settles over the pond. The stillness is
broken by the sound of evening crickets, a few
songbirds and the tinkling of our crystal goblets,
filled with sparkling Perrier and lemon.

My new lover is wearing black leather pants and a
small tightly fitted black tank top that outlines her
body perfectly. I am dressed in silk: a long white dress
with a lace-outlined V-neck, the point of which
touches my navel. A lace inlet graces my entire back
as well as inlaying the length of the long white
sleeves. The full skirt allows me complete freedom of
movement.

We are sitting at a round glass table, centered with
a lit candle and a small bouquet of freshly picked
wildflowers from the meadow. We are smiling at each
other when the waiter brings in our first
course—shrimp cocktail.

We each take turns lifting the cold pink shrimp off the side of the glass bowl and dipping it into the tangy red sauce. Carefully, my new lover brings a shrimp to my lips. I take a bite of the succulence and then she takes a bite herself. It is now my turn to offer her a first bite. We continue in this slow, lasting ritual until all the shrimp have disappeared and nightfall is comfortably settling in.

Next is salad, made fresh from the nearby garden, served on individual glass plates, topped with two artichoke hearts and accompanied with a cruet of a light garlic, oil and vinegar dressing.

After our salad, the main meal arrives: broiled pink salmon with lemon butter sauce topped with fresh dill. To its side, a mound of wild rice dressed with freshly steamed asparagus with butter adds a complement of color and taste for the meal.

As we languish after dinner in reclining chairs, sipping jasmine tea, we are given a surprise personal concert by four of the waiter's friends: a string quartet playing Brahms. They leave quietly and our waiter brings the final course before he departs for the evening.

Tall parfait glasses filled with juicy, red strawberries topped with freshly whipped cream are served to us in the library in front of a roaring fire in the large stone fireplace. A perfectly round full moon is moving over the horizon, shining through a large glass window. The chilled evening air breezes through another window as we sit together on a large, plush sectional couch. Dessert! It could take all night.

Jean

"Perfect" Body Fantasy

As I wake in my perfect body, I stretch, and feeling
no tightness or pain in my bones and muscles, look
forward to my day. I run my hands over my body,
helping to wake and invigorate the sleepy cells, and it
feels good. My body reassures me. I look out the
window, and it is beautiful outside. I look forward
with great anticipation, to my day. I wash and have
coffee, then breakfast. My breakfast is moderate, but
I don't fret over eating. There is a consciousness that
eating too much is not good for me, though, and I
feel smug in my knowledge.

I dress, choosing clothes that look good on me, not
calling undue attention to my body, but not
disguising it either. I look perfect, and I can afford to
be subtle about it. My clothes are comfortable on
me—not too tight; soft fabrics that feel good against
my skin.

I go out and move about confidently in the world,
with my head up, looking around myself at everyone,
everything. I walk with a strong, sure gait, and people
look at me with interest and respect. I get to my
workplace and am greeted warmly. I am well received
by most people, except those women who hate me for
my perfect body. I don't have to be extra-special,
extra-friendly, extra-anything to get people to like me.
My appearance does a lot of this work for me. When
I speak, everyone listens to me and laughs when I say
something funny—it doesn't even have to be very
funny. I get the response I want. I am good at my
work, and people are so appreciative. I don't have to
try to do everything—everything that other people
can't get to, everything that's left over—I just have to
be good at my job because that's what I want. And
it's good enough for everyone who matters.

I go to lunch with a couple of friends. I decide I want to eat a hearty lunch because I am pretty hungry, and I order what I want from the menu—it's a moderately large meal, though not *too* much food, and the people I am with regard my eating affectionately—I have a perfect body and I am feeding it now, doing something good for it. It is okay for me to eat. My friends and I talk about our lives—what we are doing that evening, this weekend; about our bodies, exercising, clothes, running; we gossip about other people and talk obsessively about our lovers—we are luckier than a lot of unfortunate women—we at least have lovers, even if they aren't perfect, like I am.

I am disconnected from a very large number of people in the world now. As I walk outside in the evening to make the transition to my personal life again, I am aware that the great vast hordes of beings around me are faceless, separate, not in my world. I don't know anything about them. I am a more highly evolved being than they. I am not like them. I don't want to get close to them, to know the pain of their existence. I don't want to know about it. I feel threatened somehow by them, now; though I didn't feel that threat this morning. They will hate me for my beauty, my perfect body, my privilege; they will want what I have. They will try to take it from me. The establishment society protects me. I am like them. I am what they want, what we are supposed to be. But we are not impenetrable. These "others" are many, and we are vulnerable to them in some ways. This makes me afraid and angry.

I stop to buy myself some flowers, because I deserve them (I tell myself) but I wonder if I really want them and what they mean, what they are to me. Somehow I am feeling more and more removed from the nature of living—but I'm not even able to really discern this thought, this feeling, from the vague confusion and discomfort that surfaces periodically—but which I don't acknowledge for very long.

I arrive home, check the messages on the phone machine, and decide which of them to respond to immediately. I call one of my lovers to confirm our date for that evening; then I shower and change my clothes. It is nice to have so many beautiful clothes. We meet and embrace and kiss on the street. People who see us smile approvingly because we are so lovely and deserve this privilege. The maitre'd gives us a special intimate table and treats us with respect. Everyone is so approving, and that feels good, but after a while, I feel constrained.

By the end of the evening, I am tired from being in so perfect a body, so perfect a life—because one's body is one's life, after all, so my life *must* be perfect. We should go home and make perfect love, but I just want to be alone, retreat. I don't understand why my life isn't perfect.

Carolyn Arnold

A Day Without Obsessing About Food: When Everything Is Clear

The air is filled with a touch of beginning summer; warm enough to wade barefoot in the cold ocean water. I am alone on the beach. I am walking, walking, walking along the shore. I am wearing loose and baggy clothing, and the sea breeze makes the extra material ripple gently around my body.

I pick up shells and rocks as I walk and I sing out loud. The sand stretches far in front of me. I begin to walk faster. And faster, until I am at a trot. The wind whips against my face, my hair blows back off my forehead, and the taste of salt is in my mouth. Waves break against my feet as they fall and make imprints in the sand, which the ocean laps up eagerly and sucks into her vast expense, and then licks her lips for more.

I run fast now, building momentum. Droplets of sweet sweat form on my face. It is hot now as if it were already summer. As I run I reach down and pull off my big, baggy sweatshirt in one full swoop and toss it to the sand. The air brushes against my bare breasts. I stop, only for a second to quickly shed the rest of my clothing. I am naked and I turn toward the ocean and run straight. She crashes in white-tipped waves against my shins, my knees, my thighs, my belly. She is deliciously cold. I dive into her head on and match my strength to hers, pulling back my arms and surfacing again. I float on my back and gaze into the sun as the water tingles through my naked body. And everything is clear.

Lisa Jahn-Clough

Selected Recommended Resources

Bruch, Hilda. *The Golden Cage*. New York: Vintage, 1979.

Chapkis, Wendy. *Beauty Secrets: Women and the Politics of Appearance*. Boston: South End Press, 1986.

Chernin, Kim. *The Hungry Self: Women, Eating & Identity*. New York: Harper & Row, 1985.

Chernin, Kim. *The Obsession: Reflections on the Tyranny of Slenderness*. New York: Harper Row, 1981.

Donald, C.M. *The Fat Woman Measures Up*. Charlottetown, Canada: 1986.

Freedman, Rita. *BodyLove: Learning to Like Our Looks and Ourselves*. New York: Harper & Row, 1988.

Hutchinson, Marcia Germaine. *Transforming Body Image: Learning to Love the Body You Have*. Freedom, CA: The Crossing Press, 1985.

Kano, S. *Making Peace With Food*. New York: Harper & Row, 1989.

Millman, Marcia. *Such a Pretty Face*. New York: Berkeley, 1981.

Newman, Lesléa. *Good Enough to Eat* (a novel). Ithaca, NY: Firebrand Books, 1986.

Newman, Lesléa. *Belinda's Bouquet* (children's book). Boston: Alyson Publications, 1991.

Orbach, Susie. *Fat is a Feminist Issue: The Anti-Diet Guide to Permanent Weight Loss*. New York: Berkley Books, 1978.

Orbach, Susie. *Fat is a Feminist Issue II: A Program to Conquer Compulsive Eating*. New York: Berkley Books, 1982.

Ray, Sondra. *The Only Diet There Is*. Berkeley, CA: Celestial Arts, 1981.

Roth, Geneen. *Breaking Free From Compulsive Eating*. New York: New American Library, 1984.
Roth, Geneen. *Feeding the Hungry Heart*. New York: New American Library, 1983.
Roth, Geneen. *Why Weight? A Guide to Ending Compulsive Eating*. New York: Plume, 1989.
Roth, Geneen. *When Food Is Love*. New York: New American Library, 1991.
Seid Pollack, Roberta. *Never Too Thin: Why Women Are At War With Their Bodies*. New York: Prentice Hall Press, 1989.
Schoedfielder, Lisa, and Weiser, Barb. *Shadow on a Tightrope: Writings by Women on Fat Oppression*. San Francisco: Spinters/Aunt Lute Book Company, 1983.
Székely, Éva. *Never Too Thin*. Toronto: The Women's Press, 1988.
Wolf, Naomi. *The Beauty Myth*. New York: William Morrow & Co., 1991.

Index

LESLÉA NEWMAN has been leading groups for women focusing on body image and eating patterns since 1983. Her books on the subject include a novel *Good Enough To Eat* and a children's book *Belinda's Bouquet*. Newman lives with her longtime companion in Northampton, Massachusetts.

For information about writing workshops, including "SomeBody to Love," please contact Lesléa Newman through Third Side Press.

 Third Side Press

2250 W. Farragut
Chicago, IL 60625-1802

OTHER BOOKS FROM THIRD SIDE PRESS

Cancer As a Women's Issue: Scratching the Surface, Midge Stocker, editor $10.95 1-879427-02-8

AfterShocks by Jess Wells $9.95 1-879427-08-7

The Dress/The Sharda Stories by Jess Wells $8.95 1-879427-04-4

Two Willows Chairs by Jess Wells $8.95 ISBN 1-879427-05-2

Hawkwings by Karen Lee Osborne $9.95 1-879427-00-1

On Lill Street by Lynn Kanter $10.95 1-879427-07-9

To order any of these books, or to receive a free catalog, write to us at 2250 W. Farragut, Chicago, IL 60625-1802. Please include $2 shipping for the first book and .50 for each additional book.